HAVE

CHRISTIAN EVIDENCES

YOU EVER

FOR A SKEPTICAL WORLD

WONDERED?

RUSS WHITTEN

To Vonn,
Thank you for your constant friendship, leadership, prayers, servant heart and Christian example! I am so blessed, honored and thankful to have you as a friend! Your brother in Christ,

Russ Whitten

ISBN: 978-0-89098-569-4

©2017 by 21st Century Christian

2809 12th Ave S, Nashville, TN 37204

Unless otherwise noted Scripture quotations are from the New International Version.

Scripture quotations taken from THE HOLY BIBLE, NEW INTERNATIONAL VERSION®, NIV®

Copyright © 1973, 1978, 1984, 2011 by Biblica, Inc.™

Used by permission. All rights reserved worldwide.

Cover design by Jonathan Edelhuber

Table of Contents

For my wonderful and supportive family:

Charlene, Savannah, Jackson (and Nugget) Whitten

Betty Whitten

Peggy and John David Palmer

Charles and Ellen Massey

"Always be prepared
to give an answer
to everyone
who asks you
to give the reason
for the hope
that you have."

(1 Peter 3:15)

Introduction

In the year 1880, Helen Adams Keller was born in Tuscumbia, Alabama. When Helen was only nineteen months old, a serious illness tragically left her blind and deaf, forcing this little girl to spend her childhood in a world of silent darkness. Because no one in her family could communicate with her, Helen Keller did not have the opportunity to learn about God or any type of world religion. Later, with the help of her dedicated and tenacious teacher, Anne Sullivan, Helen learned how to communicate by having someone write words on her hand with their fingers and to "listen" by feeling a speaker's face. When she was nine years old, a minister visited the Perkin's Institute for the Blind and told Helen about God. When he did, she smiled and communicated back to him these powerful words:

**"I always knew he was there,
I just didn't know his name."** [1]

How do we explain the innate feeling of God's presence in the heart of this little girl who was blind, deaf, and could not talk? Helen Keller's experience is certainly not an isolated one. Anthropologists have discovered that there seems to be a curious, universal, intuitive belief in a Supreme Being among diverse cultures from all over the world throughout known history.

Sure, there are those who say our idea of God and our "spiritual longings" simply stem from "wishful thinking" and a desire to live beyond the grave. These skeptics argue that, because people have always been haunted with the reality that life is short, confusing, painful, and often frightening, humanity invented the idea of a Higher Being in a desperate attempt to console itself. Karl Marx (1818-83) famously described these religious tendencies as "opium of the people," which serves to dull the pain of an unjust world.

However, this argument can go both ways. Couldn't it also be said that because we are haunted with the intuitive feeling of guilt when we do something wrong, some people invent the idea that there is no God so they can escape the stifling feeling of accountability? Can't it be argued that some people contrive the belief that God does not exist so that they can do whatever they please? The famed British atheist, Aldous Huxley willingly admitted this:

> I had motives for not wanting the world to have a meaning; consequently I assumed it had none, and was able, without any difficulty, to find satisfying reasons for this assumption... For myself as, no doubt, for most of my contemporaries, the philosophy of meaninglessness was essentially an instrument of liberation... We objected to the morality because it interfered with our sexual freedom..." [2]

In other words, the idea of God was putting a serious damper on his fun, so he simply deleted God from his thinking.

For most of us, however, it is not that simple. In fact, most people find these innate spiritual longings intriguing. Where do these feelings come from? Why is it that we so often encounter a vague feeling of emptiness, discontentment, and dissatisfaction —even at times when things are going well? Why is it that we all seem to have a "void within" and deep desires that nothing on this earth can ever satisfy? Isn't it interesting that we all seem to have a little voice inside that often cries out, "There's got to be more than this!"?

Sundar Singh, one of India's most famous Hindu converts to Christianity writes:

We are never satisfied with one thing for long. We always want to change our circumstances and environment. This restlessness stems from our deep inner awareness that the fleeting things of this world can never satisfy our souls, can never give us a sense of stable and unchanging fulfillment.[3]

The Greek philosopher, Plato, once described human beings as "leaky jars" suggesting that as soon as we think we have finally "filled up" our life with something that will make us content and satisfied, we slowly start to feel empty again. Why is it that each time we finally get what we thought would make us happy, we soon realize that it doesn't? We journey through life believing that just beyond the horizon we will finally find that elusive oasis of contentment, only to be disappointed by another mirage when we get there. Ravi Zacharias comments, "The loneliest moment in life is when you have just experienced what you thought would deliver the ultimate, and it has let you down."[4] This disillusionment eventually leaves us wondering—*What does make a person truly satisfied, content, fulfilled and happy?*

Have you ever wondered if these feelings are actually trying to tell us something? Could it be that these strange "spiritual longings" might be clues pointing to something we have yet to discover?

This book is essentially an attempt to address these questions. In it, we will explore the big questions of life and, specifically, the truth claims of the Christian faith. My goal is to present a case that the Christian faith is not only true, but that it is immensely attractive, profoundly relevant and extremely satisfying.

CHAPTER 1

What Is
the Meaning of Life?

"...we all have a fundamental dis-ease.
It is an unquenchable fire that renders the vast majority of us
incapable in this life of ever coming to full peace...all great
literature, poetry, art, philosophy, psychology, and religion
tries to name and analyze this longing."
~ Huston Smith

T he story is told of four brothers who had each become successful and wealthy. They were sitting around on New Year's Eve discussing the Christmas gifts they had been able to give to their elderly mother who lived far away in another city. The first brother boasted, "This Christmas, I was able to buy our dear mother a large, seven-bedroom house." The second brother proudly added, "I was able to build mother a movie theater that can seat fifty of her friends in this new house." The third brother bragged, "I was able to purchase a brand new Mercedes for dear mother and had it delivered to her on Christmas Eve." The three brothers then asked the fourth, "What did you get mother for Christmas?" The fourth brother replied, "You know how Mom has always loved reading the Bible and, because of her failing eyesight, she can't read anymore? Well, I recently found out about a parrot that could recite the entire Bible. It took ten preachers five years to train it. I had to pay $100,000 to buy it, but it was worth it. All mother has to do now is just name the chapter and the verse and the parrot will recite it." The other brothers were truly impressed.

After the holidays, the mother sent "thank you" letters to each of her four sons, which said the following:

Dear Milton,

The house you built for me is too large! I live in only one room, but I have to clean the whole entire house. Thanks a lot!

Dear Markus,

You gave me an expensive movie theater that can seat fifty friends. You seemed to forget that all my friends are dead! I've lost my hearing and I'm nearly blind. I'll never use it. Thank you for the gesture, just the same.

Dear Marvin,

I am too old to drive. I stay home and have my groceries delivered, so I will never use the Mercedes. Thanks, just the same.

Dearest Melvin,

You were the only son to have the good sense to give a little thought to your gift. The chicken was delicious!

This story brings up the following questions: "Is there any gift that can truly satisfy?" "Is there anything in this world that can bring lasting happiness, joy, contentment, and meaning?" In this life, it seems that true contentment is always just around the next corner, over the next hill, somewhere over the rainbow, always just out of our reach. It is to be found in the next thing, the next purchase, the next job, the next relationship, the next experience, the next year or the next place. All this leaves us wondering:

Where can real, lasting contentment, and meaning be found?

I would like to address this vital question by looking at one of the great books in the Bible, the book of Ecclesiastes. Ecclesiastes is a book about experimentation. It is the personal diary of a man who is reflecting on his lifelong quest to find what brings a person lasting contentment, meaning, and joy in life. The author, a seemingly grumpy, sour, old man, looks back over the years of his life and, in essence, rolls his eyes and grumbles, "been there, done that." He has experimented and purposefully tasted everything life has to offer. He has tried everything under the sun to find meaning and happiness. He's tried education, intellectualism, pleasure, wealth, power, fame, success, work, grand accomplishments, and a bunch of relationships. He has left no stone unturned in his robust quest to find the meaning of life. Here is his report in a nutshell:

> "Meaningless! Meaningless!" says the Teacher. "Utterly meaningless! Everything is meaningless." (Ecclesiastes 1:2)

That's a real "pick me up" verse, isn't it? If you are looking for the meaning of life, the book of Ecclesiastes, initially, might not seem too promising. The first several chapters sound downright pessimistic, dreary, and depressing. However, if you read all twelve chapters of this ancient book carefully, you will see that the author actually has the answer, but before he gives it to us, he spends most of the book telling us where we will *not* find lasting contentment and ultimate happiness. Thus, before we look at what the author of Ecclesiastes says about the meaning of life, let's look at how he answers the question,

"What does not bring meaning, peace and joy to life?"

"I would be happy if I were more educated!"

Many people throughout history have felt that education, wisdom, and knowledge are the keys to a meaningful and joyful life. In the first chapter of the book of Ecclesiastes, the author writes about his experiment with wisdom and education.

> "I, the Teacher, was king over Israel in Jerusalem. I applied

my mind to study and to explore by wisdom all that is done under the heavens... I said to myself, 'Look, I have increased in wisdom more than anyone who has ruled over Jerusalem before me; I have experienced much of wisdom and knowledge.'" (Ecclesiastes 1:12-16)

Traditionally, most have taken the position that the author of Ecclesiastes was none other than Solomon, the notoriously wise, wealthy, powerful son of David and King of Israel. Let's look for a moment at how wise and educated King Solomon was according to the Bible:

"God gave Solomon wisdom and very great insight and a breadth of understanding as measureless as the sand on the seashore. Solomon's wisdom was greater than the wisdom of all the men of the East, and greater than all the wisdom of Egypt. He was wiser than anyone else... And his fame spread to all the surrounding nations. He spoke three thousand proverbs and his songs numbered a thousand and five. He spoke about plant life, from the cedar of Lebanon to the hyssop that grows out of walls. He also taught about animals and birds, reptiles and fish. From all nations people came to listen to Solomon's wisdom, sent by all the kings of the world, who had heard of his wisdom." (1 Kings 4:29-34)

"When the queen of Sheba saw all the wisdom of Solomon...she was overwhelmed... She said to the king, 'The report I heard in my own country about your achievements and your wisdom is true. But I did not believe these things until I came and saw with my own eyes. Indeed, not even half was told me; in wisdom and wealth you have far exceeded the report I heard. How happy your people must be! How happy your officials, who continually stand before you and hear your wisdom!'" (1 Kings 10:4-8)

So, the writer of Ecclesiastes was the smartest of the smart, the astutest of the astute and the cleverest of the clever. He had reached the pinnacle of acumen, knowledge, education, and intelligence. He was sophisticated, well-read, scholarly, erudite, refined, distinguished, and cultured. If ever there was a test case to see if knowledge, wisdom, and education hold the keys to contentment and true happiness, Solomon is our man. Yet, here is his report on the matter:

> "I, the Teacher, was king over Israel in Jerusalem. I applied my mind to study and to explore by wisdom all that is done under the heavens... I have seen all the things that are done under the sun; all of them are meaningless, a chasing after the wind. ...I said to myself, 'Look, I have increased in wisdom more than anyone who has ruled over Jerusalem before me; I have experienced much of wisdom and knowledge.' Then I applied myself to the understanding of wisdom, and also of madness and folly, but I learned that this, too, is a chasing after the wind. For with much wisdom comes much sorrow; the more knowledge, the more grief." (Ecclesiastes 1:12-18)

Albert Einstein, two days before his death, said something very similar:

> "Those of us who know the most are gloomiest about the future."[5]

The message here is not that education and knowledge are unimportant. Solomon affirms this in Ecclesiastes 2:13, "I saw that wisdom is better than folly, just as light is better than darkness." The point is that lasting contentment and ultimate meaning cannot be found in wisdom, knowledge, and education.

"What about pleasure, partying, and fun? Will these things bring me real contentment and meaning?"

In the second chapter of Ecclesiastes, we read about Solomon's experiment with pleasure and fun: "I denied myself nothing my eyes desired; I refused my heart no pleasure" (Ecclesiastes 2:10). Can you imagine? Anything he saw that he wanted, he took. Anything he wanted to do, he did. Anywhere he wanted to go, he went.

Furthermore, we learn elsewhere in the Old Testament that King Solomon "loved many foreign women... Solomon held fast to them in love. He had seven hundred wives of royal birth and three hundred concubines." (1 Kings 11:1-3) Wow! Surely, all these relationships brought him contentment. Surely, all the fun and pleasure that he experienced brought happiness—or did it?

The Irish writer, Oscar Wilde once said the following:

"In this world there are two great tragedies: One is not getting what you want, and the other is getting it."[6]

The book of Ecclesiastes chronicles the outcome of getting everything you want. The author eventually comes to the same conclusion as Oscar Wilde:

"I said to myself, 'Come now, I will test you with pleasure to find out what is good.' But that also proved to be meaningless." (Ecclesiastes 2:1)

The truth is that pleasure is always temporary, momentary and short lived. It has no staying power. The writer of the New Testament book of Hebrews commends Moses for his faith:

"By faith Moses, when he had grown up, refused to be known as the son of Pharaoh's daughter. He chose to be mistreated along with the people of God *rather than to enjoy the fleeting pleasures of sin*. He regarded disgrace for the sake of Christ as of greater value than the treasures of Egypt, because he was looking ahead to his reward." (Hebrews 11:24-26)

As the adopted son of Pharaoh's daughter, Moses could have had everything Egypt had to offer, but he chose God rather than the fleeting "pleasures of sin" because he knew that the world's treasures could not ultimately provide life, satisfaction, meaning, peace, or joy. Of course, not all fun and pleasure is sinful. However, Solomon seems to be warning us that even a bold pursuit for the good, non-sinful pleasures of life can still lead us down a dead end street, ultimately leaving us with a strange feeling of emptiness. This is addressed in an interesting verse (also attributed to Solomon) found in the book of Proverbs:

"If you find honey, eat just enough—too much of it, and you will vomit." (Proverbs 25:16)

In other words, even good, wholesome things, in excess, can eventually make you sick. Ravi Zacharias summed it up this way, "Any pleasure, however good, if not kept in balance, will distort reality and destroy appetite... I am absolutely convinced that meaninglessness does not come from being weary of pain; meaninglessness comes from being weary of pleasure."[7] [8] This is precisely the conclusion articulated in Ecclesiastes.

Interestingly, Jesus taught that to find life we must do exactly the opposite of what Solomon tried. Solomon, trying to find life, "denied himself nothing" and found nothing. Jesus, on the other hand, promised "deny yourself and follow me" and you will find life (Matthew 16:24-26).

"I would be happy, if I were rich!"

It has been said, "The things that really matter in life are not things." Most of us would readily agree with this. Even so, a lot of us still identify with and share the attitude of Tevya, the main character of *Fiddler on the Roof*: "What's so wrong with being rich?" he inquired. "Money is the world's curse!" —came the response. Then looking to the heavens, Tevya prayed, "Then may the Lord smite me with it and may I never recover!"

When Tevya sings his famous song, *"If I were a Rich Man,"* it is obvious that he wholeheartedly believes that *if* he were a rich man, *then* he would finally be happy and content. What would King Solomon, by far the wealthiest man in the world in his day, have to say to Tevya (and us) about trying to find contentment in money? Before we hear what he would say, let's briefly look at just how rich Solomon was according to the Bible.

"The weight of the gold that Solomon received yearly was 666 talents (25 tons) not including the revenues from merchants and traders and from all the Arabian kings and the governors of the territories." (1 Kings 10:14-15)

"King Solomon was greater in riches and wisdom than all the other kings of the earth." (1 Kings 10:23)

"I bought male and female slaves and had other slaves who were born in my house. I also owned more herds and flocks than anyone in Jerusalem before me. I amassed silver and gold for myself, and the treasure of kings and provinces. I acquired male and female singers, and a harem as well—the delights of a man's heart. I became greater by far than anyone in Jerusalem before me...." (Ecclesiastes 2:7-9)

"Solomon's daily provisions were thirty cors (about 185 bushels or 6.6 kiloliters) of the finest flour and sixty cors (about 375 bushels or 13.2 kiloliters) of meal, ten head of stall-fed cattle, twenty of pasture-fed cattle and a hundred sheep and goats, as well as deer, gazelles, roebucks and choice fowl... Solomon had four thousand stalls for chariot horses, and twelve thousand horses. The district officers, each in his month, supplied provisions for King Solomon and all who came to the king's table. They saw to it that nothing was lacking." (1 Kings 4:22-27)

To put this into perspective, it should be pointed out that Solomon's "daily provisions" would have been enough to feed 10,000 people! Again, if there was ever a test case to see if money, riches, and wealth could bring happiness and contentment to a person, it would be this guy. However, as Solomon reflects over the years of his affluent, comfortable, charmed life, here is his report on the matter:

"Whoever loves money never has money enough; whoever loves wealth is never satisfied with his income. This too is meaningless." (Ecclesiastes 5:10)

Time and time again, we see this truth played out in the lives of the rich and famous. For example, someone once asked John D. Rockefeller, the richest man of his time, "How much money is enough?" He replied with a perfect definition of greed: "Just a little more." A real estate tycoon said something similar: "I don't want all the land in the world, just whatever touches mine."[9]

Perhaps one of the most famous illustrations that money can't buy happiness is the fascinating story of Howard Hughes (1905-1976):

> At age 45, Howard Hughes was one of the most glamorous men in America. He dated Hollywood actresses, piloted exotic test aircraft, and worked on top-secret CIA contracts. He owned a string of hotels around the world, even an airline—TWA—to carry him on global jaunts. Twenty years later, at age 65, Howard Hughes still had plenty of money—$2.3 billion to be exact. But the world's richest man had become one of its most pathetic. He lived in small dark rooms atop his hotels. Without sun and without joy. He was unkempt: a scraggly beard had grown waist-length, his hair fell down his back, his fingernails were two inches long. His once-powerful 6'4" frame had shrunk to about 100 pounds. This famous and powerful man spent most of his time watching movies over and over, with the same movie showing as many as 150 times. He lay naked in bed, deathly afraid of germs. Life held no meaning for him. Finally, emaciated and hooked on drugs, he died at age 67, for a lack of a medical device his own company had helped to develop.[10]

The sad story of Howard Hughes is far from unique. Why is it that the wealthiest people of the world are so often the most miserable? Why is it that the World Health Organization reports that the countries with the greatest Gross National Product are the nations with the highest suicide rate? Why is it that the "have nots" of the world consistently exhibit more contentment and joy than the "have so much they don't know what to do with it" people of the world?

Perhaps, the answer is summed up well by a Chinese billionaire who recently converted to the Christian faith. "Why did you convert to Christianity?" he was asked. His intriguing answer was this: "All my life I have spent my time climbing the mountain of wealth and success and when I finally got to the top, I looked around and nothing was there."

Solomon's message is clear: Money and riches cannot bring life, meaning, peace, joy, or even security. The wisdom of Ecclesiastes is that a rich life is not getting everything you want, but enjoying everything you have.

Thus far, Solomon has addressed three "classic proposed solutions" to finding meaning in life. He has experimented with intellectualism, hedonism, and materialism and has found each to be a meaningless pursuit resulting in a sense of emptiness, rather than real joy.

"What about good old fashioned hard work, success, and accomplishments? Can't these things bring contentment?"

Amazingly, Solomon's extravagant lifestyle did not make him lazy. In fact, in another failed attempt to find contentment, the writer of Ecclesiastes became a workaholic.

> "I undertook great projects: I built houses for myself and planted vineyards. I made gardens and parks and planted all kinds of fruit trees in them. I made reservoirs to water groves of flourishing trees." (Ecclesiastes 2:4-6)

> "...My heart took delight in all my labor, and this was the reward for all my toil. Yet when I surveyed all that my hands had done and what I had toiled to achieve, everything was meaningless, a chasing after the wind; nothing was gained under the sun." (Ecclesiastes 2:10-11)

> "So I hated life, because the work that is done under the sun was grievous to me. All of it is meaningless, a chasing after the wind. I hated all the things I had toiled for under the sun...." (Ecclesiastes 2:17-18)

> "...I saw that all toil and all achievement spring from one person's envy of another. This too is meaningless, a chasing after the wind." (Ecclesiastes 4:4)

In an interview with the BBC, Sting, one of the most successful, influential, and talented musicians of our time, commented, "I thought success and happiness were the same thing, but when I was at my most successful, I was most unhappy."[11]

Most of us will never experience the staggering level of achievement, success, and accomplishment as people like Solomon or Sting, but isn't it interesting to hear that even if we could, contentment and lasting happiness would still elude us?

One of the more memorable commentaries on the transitory nature of "kingdom building" is found in a sonnet by Percy Bysshe Shelley (1792-1822) published in 1818 entitled *Ozymandias*. This poem speaks of a traveler passing through a desolate, barren stretch of desert who comes across a giant, ancient statue of Ozymandias (another name for Ramesses the Great, Pharaoh of the nineteenth dynasty of Egypt). This once impressive statue of the long-dead Egyptian "king of kings" now lies broken in pieces, half sunk in the bleak desert sand. On the base of the statue, these proud words are inscribed:

> *"My name is Ozymandias, King of Kings:*
> *Look upon my works, ye Mighty, and despair!"*

The traveler in the poem then "looks upon his works" and comments:

> *Nothing beside remains. Round the decay*
> *Of that colossal wreck, boundless and bare*
> *The lone and level sands stretch far away.*

Shelley's famous poem skillfully echoes the message of Ecclesiastes: All the great works of humankind are short-lived and will one day be subject to decay.

What about fame or reaching the top of your game—will these things provide contentment?

After winning his second Wimbledon, tennis great Boris Becker stunned the world when he spoke with reporters about his daily battle with emptiness and hopelessness, which almost led to suicide. He said, "I had won Wimbledon twice before, once as the youngest player. I was rich. I had all the material possessions I needed: money, cars, women, everything… I know that this is a cliché. It's the old song of the movie and pop stars who commit suicide. They have everything, and yet they are so unhappy… I had no inner peace. I was a puppet on a string." [12]

During an interview with Diane Sawyer on ABC's "Primetime Live," actor/director Mel Gibson discussed the reasons he turned back to God and initially began meditating on "The Passion of the Christ." "Let's face it," said Gibson, "I have been to the pinnacle of what secular utopia has to offer. I got money, fame, this, that and the other… It wasn't enough. It's not good enough. It leaves you empty. The more you eat, the emptier you get." [13]

At the time of his death, Freddie Mercury, the flamboyant, lead singer of the British rock group *Queen*, was one of the richest, most admired, and famous men in the world. After all, he was the leader of one of the most internationally popular rock bands in history. In an interview just before his death in 1991, he admitted that he was desperately lonely and lamented, "You can have everything in the world and still be the loneliest man, and that is the most bitter type of loneliness. Success has brought me world idolization and millions of pounds, but it's prevented me from having the one thing we all need—a loving, ongoing relationship." [14]

In one of Freddie Mercury's last recorded songs, he cried out the lyrics: "Does anybody know what we are living for?"

This will be the question we address in our next chapter.

CHAPTER 2

What Gives
Our Lives Joy?

"So now, from this mad passion
Which made me take art for an idol and a king
I have learnt the burden of error that it bore
And what misfortune springs from man's desire...
The world's frivolities have robbed me of the time
That I was given for reflecting upon God."
~ **Michelangelo (1475-1564)**

"He has also set eternity in the human heart..."
(Ecclesiastes 3:11)

Socrates once said, "the unexamined life is not worth living." As we saw in the previous chapter, the author of Ecclesiastes certainly could not be accused of living an unexamined life. In fact, he spends most of his book examining his past and reflecting on his mistakes. He basically says, "I've tried everything under the sun to find meaning. I've tried education, pleasure, money, power, fame, work, accomplishments and a bunch of relationships, and I can tell you, from firsthand experience, that if you are trying to find meaning and contentment in those things, you are heading down a dead end street." Solomon had experienced all the things we typically think are supposed to bring happiness and his conclusion is that these things, especially in excessive abundance, will ultimately leave you empty. He concludes that most people are desperately searching for meaning, peace, and contentment, but are constantly looking in the wrong places. All this, drives us to the question...

"Okay then, what *does* bring contentment, joy, peace, and meaning to our lives?"

The writer of Ecclesiastes answers this important question in two ways. First, in the midst of his gloomy report on his lifelong quest for meaning, which for the most part, is filled with valuable information about where we will *not* find contentment, he cleverly sprinkles in verses throughout the book that offer at least part of the answer. This partial answer can be summed up in the following words:

Enjoy today! Don't postpone joy!

Consider the following verses that create an interesting thread throughout the book of Ecclesiastes:

"A person can do nothing better than to eat and drink and find satisfaction in their own toil. This too, I see, is from the hand of God, for without him, who can eat or find enjoyment?" (Ecclesiastes 2:24-25)

"I know that there is nothing better for people than to be happy and to do good while they live. That each of them may eat and drink, and find satisfaction in all their toil—this is the gift of God." (Ecclesiastes 3:12-13)

"So I saw that there is nothing better for a person than to enjoy their work, because this is their lot. For who can bring them to see what will happen after them?" (Ecclesiastes 3:22)

"This is what I have observed to be good: that it is appropriate for a person to eat, to drink, and to find satisfaction in their toilsome labor under the sun during the few days of life God has given them—for this is their lot." (Ecclesiastes 5:18)

"So I commend the enjoyment of life, because there is nothing better for a person under the sun than to eat and drink and be glad. Then joy will accompany them in that toil all the days of the life God has given them under the sun." (Ecclesiastes 8:15)

"Go, eat your food with gladness, and drink your wine with a joyful heart, for God has already approved what you do. Always be clothed in white, and always anoint your head with oil. Enjoy life with your wife, whom you love...." (Ecclesiastes 9:7-9)

Where can we find meaning and joy in the world? I believe we have some answers here, and they almost sound too simple. The writer of Ecclesiastes basically says, "Look around you! Look at the blessings God has given you today. Enjoy these blessings! Be glad and thankful about them. Don't postpone joy!"

A few years ago, there was a popular Kodak commercial in which a seemingly exasperated mother was desperately trying to get herself and her kids ready to go somewhere. These three happy, energetic, rambunctious children were holding up progress every step of the way with pillow fights, jumping on the bed, dancing, and simply enjoying life. Finally, a smile came on the mother's tired face. She shook her head, grabbed a camera, and snapped a picture of her giggling, adorable, happy kids. The narrator's voice then said, "Stop. Look around. This is the good stuff. Don't miss it!" This commercial summed up well one of the most important lessons from the book of Ecclesiastes, which is perhaps best encapsulated in Psalm 118:24:

"This is the day the Lord has made; let us rejoice and be glad in it" (ESV).

The Jewish Talmud, which is the collected wisdom of the early rabbis, echoes this sentiment, stating, "In the world to come, each of us will be called to account for all the good things God put on earth which we refused to enjoy." In other words, God does not simply *allow* us to enjoy the present moments of life; He *desires* it.

Why don't we enjoy today?

There are two main reasons that Solomon knows will keep a lot of us from enjoying today. First of all, some of us are not going to enjoy today because we are too consumed with living in the past and longing for "the good old days." So, Solomon shares this simple, straightforward admonishment: "Do not say, 'Why were the old days better than these?' For it is not wise to ask such questions" (Ecclesiastes 7:10). It is so easy to completely miss today's blessings because we are too busy complaining about the terrible state of the world and romanticizing about the way things used to be.

Second, Solomon also knows that some people are not going to enjoy today because they are too busy living for or worrying about tomorrow. He knows that too many people consistently live with the misguided idea that, "When _____ happens, then I'll be content and happy." John Lennon once said, "Life is what's happening while we're busy making other plans." Jesus had a lot to say about this and taught His followers, "Do not worry about tomorrow, for tomorrow will worry about itself. Each day has enough trouble of its own" (Matthew 6:34). Someone once condensed their life this way:

"I used to be dying to get out of college.

Then I was dying to get married.

Then I was dying to get a good job.

Then I was dying to get a promotion.

Then I was dying to get the kids off to college.

Then I was dying to retire.

Now, I'm dying and I realize that I forgot to live."

In the book of Ecclesiastes, Solomon comes to the conclusion that joy, meaning, peace, contentment and life can't be found in pleasure, prosperity, or power. He also comes to the realization that these things can't be found in dwelling in the past or living for the future. He does discover, however, that every single day, even the incredibly difficult ones, has its blessings. The author of

Ecclesiastes reminds us that the happiest people are the ones who have gratitude for what they have, despite their circumstances. They are the ones who refuse to let the things they can't control destroy what that can enjoy.[15] This attitude is beautifully summed up in the following poem:

THIS MOMENT

I may never see tomorrow; there's no written guarantee,
And the things that happened yesterday belong to history,
I cannot predict the future, I cannot change the past,
I have just the present moment, I must treat it as my last,
I must use this moment wisely for it soon will pass away,
And be lost to me forever as part of yesterday,
I must exercise compassion, help the fallen to their feet,
Be a friend unto the friendless, make an empty life complete,
The unkind things I do today may never be undone,
And friendships that I fail to win may nevermore be won,
I may not have another chance on bended knee to pray,
And thank God with humble heart for giving me this day.

~ Author Unknown

The message that we need to learn to "enjoy now" is a good one, but would be tragically hollow without Solomon's final conclusion, to which we will now turn our attention.

It has been said that the book of Ecclesiastes is for people who want to know what life without God looks like. Indeed, Solomon can be seen as a test case for life apart from God, and his book is full of wisdom about how *not* to live. He has chronicled a systematic search for an alternative path to life's meaning—a life without the Creator—and has come up empty. All this has driven him to the conclusion that to find meaning, joy, peace, and life we must look outside of ourselves and search for answers "beyond the sun." Fortunately, the writer of Ecclesiastes does not leave us wallowing in his despair and in the end offers us the answer to the question of life's meaning. In Ecclesiastes 12, we see the finale of Solomon's lifelong quest for meaning and joy in life. He finally comes to the profound conclusion that the reason we are not satisfied, content and happy here is because we aren't supposed to be. He wants us to realize that God has designed us to be empty, frustrated, and discontented without Him and that we were meant for far more than simply this short life "under the sun." He wants us to know that this world is not our home and that we were created to live forever in heaven, not in this fallen world. Thus, he explains that God has planted in every human heart a yearning and a longing for heaven, saying, "He has made everything beautiful in its time. He has also set eternity in the human heart..." (Ecclesiastes 3:11). It is like the story of a little boy flying a kite on a foggy and cloudy day. A man walked up beside him, gazed into the thick fog and inquired, "What are you doing?" "I'm flying my kite," said the boy. The man asked, "How do you know it's there?" The little boy responded, "I can feel the tug!"

Solomon is trying to get us to understand that deep down in our souls, we all feel the tug of heaven, and we intuitively know that we were made for more than this messed up world. That is why in every human heart there is a hunger that nothing on this earth can truly satisfy. The seventeenth century French mathematician, Blaise Pascal (1623-1662) came to the same conclusion and provided the following well-known quotation:

> "Happiness is neither within nor without us—it is in God and only when God is in us is happiness within and without us... All of us have been created with a God shaped vacuum that only God can fill."

It should be pointed out that God does not disapprove of our pursuit of happiness. We are told in the Bible, however, that God does take offense when we pursue happiness in the wrong places. Over and over, we are reminded that when we seek to find lasting fulfillment in anything other than God, we will instead find emptiness, frustration, and meaninglessness. Thus, God asks humanity this question, "Why spend money on what is not bread, and your labor on what does not satisfy? Listen, listen to me, and eat what is good, and you will delight in the richest of fare. Give ear and come to me; hear me, that your soul may live" (Isaiah 55:2-3). In other words, God asks us, "Why do you always try to fill up your emptiness and quench your thirst for meaning with things that will not ultimately satisfy? Why do you keep hurting yourselves? If you want happiness, why are you going down this road?"

The book of Ecclesiastes attempts to explain to us that life without God is empty, we will never find infinite answers in finite things, we will never find ultimate meaning in life "under the sun," we are not fully home here and we will not genuinely enjoy life until we learn to enjoy God. This profound message runs throughout the Bible, as we see in verses like Psalm 37:4: "Take delight in the LORD, and he will give you the desires of your heart." In the end, Solomon finally points us to the One who can give life meaning. Ecclesiastes ends with the following conclusion. Here, suggests the teacher, is the meaning of life. Here is the recipe to a good, full, content life:

> ### "Now all has been heard;
> ### here is the conclusion of the matter:
> ### Fear God and keep his commandments,
> ### for this is the whole duty of man."
> ### (Ecclesiastes 12:13)

Solomon doesn't even try to be fancy about it. If you want contentment, meaning, and joy in life that surpasses understanding, there are two musts: Take God seriously, and do what He says. He would also add, the younger we realize this, the better. "Remember your Creator in the days of your youth," the teacher counsels, "before the days of trouble come and the years approach when you will say, 'I find no pleasure in them'" (Ecclesiastes 12:1). In other words, the best time to start living for God is *right now*, especially if you are young. In one of the most curious verses in the Old Testament, the author of Ecclesiastes writes, "If a snake bites before it is charmed, the charmer receives no fee" (Ecclesiastes 10:11). What does this strange verse mean? Let's put it this way: If you happen to be a snake charmer, when is the best time to start charming your snake? Certainly, one good answer is, "Before it bites you!" With this in mind, if you are a young person, when is the best time to start living for God? Without a doubt, the best answer is, "Before you get hurt."

Solomon seems to be saying, "Start living for God *right now*, before you become a bitter, cynical, empty, old person full of regrets, addictions, embarrassing memories, and bad habits. Embrace God while you're young, before you have a string of failed, immoral relationships and haunted by 'what might have been if I'd only been faithful to God earlier in life.'" Way back, in Genesis 4:7, God told Cain, "sin is crouching at your door; it desires to have you, but you must rule over it." In other words, you've got to charm the snake, before it bites.

In many ways, the book of Ecclesiastes raises more questions than it answers. It describes life "under the sun" as short, meaningless, empty, monotonous, wearisome, unpredictable, difficult, and often unfair. Yet, the book can be seen as an important sign post pointing forward to the rest of the Bible where the central message is that real life consists in more than the few years we spend on this earth. It has been said that Ecclesiastes is the question to which Christ is the answer. Indeed, millions upon millions throughout history and all over the globe have discovered and experienced that only Jesus Christ can fill the God shaped void in the human heart. One writer said this about

Jesus' ability to satisfy a person's spiritual hunger:

> "On the surface we seem quite different; but deep down we are
> fundamentally the same—We are all desperately unhappy about
> something—and we don't know what it is. In every person there
> is this nameless, unsatisfied longing; this vague discontent; this
> something lacking; this frustration; this something that only
> Jesus Christ can satisfy."[16]

The apostle John could not have been more concise or explicit about this truth, saying, "Whoever has the Son has life; whoever does not have the Son of God does not have life" (1 John 5:12). In other words, ultimately, only Jesus Christ can fill a person's spiritual hunger and thirst. In Christ, the hunger and thirst disappear, and the human heart at last finds that for which it has been searching: peace, hope, joy, forgiveness, meaning, and life.

C.S. Lewis once noted, "Our heavenly father has provided many delightful inns for us along our journey, but he takes great care to see that we do not mistake any of them for home." Ultimately, Solomon came to realize this to be true. He had been blessed with the opportunity to visit many of life's "delightful inns" and had learned that when these precious moments come along, it is wise to enjoy them with fully a grateful heart. All the while, however, a gnawing sense of homesickness for a place he had never been haunted him like an echo of an enchanting tune he had never heard. At the end of Solomon's lifelong quest for meaning, it finally seems to dawn on him that this seemingly unexplainable homesickness can be best explained as a hint of another world—our real home—and these faint echoes can be seen as clues to life's meaning. He finally realized that he had lived most of his life with his back to the light and his eyes lustfully fixated on the glittering things upon which the light fell. In the end, he wisely counsels us to turn from the world's shiny, sparkling, fleeting pleasures that consistently fail to deliver contentment and "trace the rays of light back to their source."[17]

It would be difficult to find a more eloquent conclusion to

this chapter than the following thoughts by Oxford University Professor Alister McGrath:

"Many have found that the awesome sight of the star-studded heavens evoke a sense of wonder, an awareness of transcendence, that is charged with spiritual significance. Yet the distant shimmering of stars does not itself create this sense of longing; it merely exposes what is already there. They are catalysts for our spiritual insights, revealing our emptiness and compelling us to ask whether and how this void might be filled.

Might our true origins and destiny somehow lie beyond those stars? Might there not be a homeland, from which we are presently exiled and to which we secretly long to return? Might not our accumulation of discontentment and disillusionment with our present existence be a pointer to another land where our true destiny lies and which is able to make its presence felt now in this haunting way?

Suppose that this is not where we are meant to be but that a better land is at hand? We don't belong here. We have somehow lost our way. Would not this make our present existence both strange and splendid? Strange, because it is not where our true destiny lies; splendid, because it points ahead to where that real hope might be found. The beauty of the night skies or a glorious sunset are important pointers to the origins and the ultimate fulfillment of our heart's deepest desires. But if we mistake the signpost for what is signposted, we will attach our hopes and longings to lesser goals, which cannot finally quench our thirst for meaning." [18]

CHAPTER 3

How Did the Universe Begin?

Augustine of Hippo (354-430 A.D.) once wrote, "You [God] have made us for yourself and our hearts are restless until they find their rest in you."[19] Augustine, along with millions and millions of others from every nation, language, generation and race, discovered that in God we can finally find that for which the human heart has been longing—contentment, peace, hope, stability, security, meaning, forgiveness, and life. Still, there are many who wonder, "Can it be real?" How do we know God really exists? Obviously, this is one of life's ultimate questions with which every person must wrestle. Mortimer Adler, the co-editor of *Encyclopedia Britannica* once suggested, "More consequences for thought and action follow from the affirmation or denial of God than from answering any other question." In the next few chapters, we are going to look at reasons to believe that God exists. There have traditionally been three basic arguments used for reasons to believe in the existence of God:

1) **Whatever begins to exist must have a cause. The universe began to exist. Therefore, the universe must have a cause.**[20]

2) **Every complex design that serves a purpose has a designer. The universe, earth and its inhabitants display mind-boggling complexity in design. Thus, there must be an Intelligent Designer.**[21]

3) **Objective moral values can exist only if God exists. Objective moral values do exist. Therefore, God must exist.**

In this chapter, we will look at Reason #1.

EVERYTHING THAT HAS A BEGINNING HAS A CAUSE

Where did our universe come from?

When we consider the origin of the universe, we are left with three possible options:

1. **The universe is eternal.**
2. **The universe just popped into existence, out of nothing.**
3. **The universe was created.**

For the rest of this chapter, we will carefully explore each of these options:

1. IS THE UNIVERSE ETERNAL?

What evidence do we have that the universe is not eternal?

A. The Expanding Universe

Up until the 1920s, the prevailing view of most astronomers was that the universe had always existed, the Milky Way galaxy made up the entire cosmos, and the universe was static (neither expanding or contracting). All this dramatically changed in 1924 on the summit of Mount Wilson in Southern California, when the American astronomer, Edwin Hubble (1883-1953), peering through the just-completed Hooker Telescope, observed hazy blobs of light that were far too distant to be part of the Milky Way. He eventually proved that these faint lights were, in fact, other entire galaxies, revealing that the universe goes well beyond the Milky Way. It wasn't long after this that Hubble made another amazing discovery. For years scientists had noticed that distant stars seemed to be "redder" than other stars. As early as 1842, Christian Andreas Doppler had pointed out that just as a sound's pitch seems to drop when it gets farther away, a distant light's color would seem to change when it traveled farther away. Could it be that these distant galaxies in space seem to be "redder" because they are constantly moving away from earth? Could it be that the universe is not static, but rapidly expanding and becoming larger with every passing second? This was precisely the conclusion Edwin Hubble reached as he discovered that the farther out in space you go, the faster things are moving away from Earth. His analysis led to the first observational support that the universe actually did have an explosive beginning. Science teachers will often draw several dots on a balloon and blow it up to illustrate our expanding universe and the way galaxies continually move away from one another. The fact that our universe expands this way suggests that if you could "rewind a video" of the history of our universe, you would see the galaxies getting closer and closer to one another until they finally converged at a central point of origin, a dense initial state that astronomers would later call a *singularity*. The implications of this discovery were staggering. Would not a central point of origin suggest that the universe definitely had a beginning? Furthermore, wouldn't a beginning suggest a Beginner or a Creator? In his book entitled *The God Hypothesis*, Michael A. Corey writes, "By far the most important piece of evidence supporting the existence of a Divine Creator is the relatively recent scientific discovery of a definite beginning to the universe."[22]

B. Cosmic Microwave Background Radiation

In 1965, Robert Wilson and Arno Penzias were testing an ultra-sensitive microwave radiation detector at Bell Laboratories in Holmdel, New Jersey, and kept encountering a background hissing noise they could not explain. At first, they thought this unwanted noise must have been caused by a malfunction on their antenna. Sure enough, upon close inspection they found that their instrument had pigeon droppings on it (which Penzias described in his report as "white dielectric material"). However, even after the giant horn-shaped antenna was thoroughly cleaned, no matter where they pointed it into space, they continued to pick up an irritating low-grade "hum." Penzias and Wilson then learned that for several years astronomers had been working on the theory that microwave background radiation would be expected if an explosion was the beginning point of the universe. Could it be, it was eventually proposed, that the antenna is not malfunctioning after all, but is actually picking up low-level thermal radiation "after glow" left over from some past cosmic catastrophe or explosion? As it turned out, in 1978, Penzias and Wilson were awarded the Nobel Prize in physics for their accidental discovery of Cosmic Microwave Background Radiation, which provided significant proof that the universe did, in fact, have a beginning and offered the first hard evidence to support the Big Bang theory. After winning the Nobel Prize, Arno Penzias would later say, "The best data we have (concerning the Big Bang) are exactly what I would have predicted, had I nothing to go on but the five books of Moses, the Psalms, the Bible as a whole."

What are the implications of this discovery? What caused this first explosion? Think about it this way: Suppose that you are a parent of a rambunctious little boy and, all of a sudden, you hear a small explosion in your house. Concerned, you shout to your child, "What was that?" Immediately, your child yells, "Nothing! It just happened!"

Would you...

A. ...say to yourself, "Hmm? That's strange. Oh well, if my child says 'it just happened' then I guess I'll accept that and assume that the small explosion did not have a cause."

OR...

B. ...run upstairs, look for (and punish) the cause?

There is now abundant scientific evidence that the universe came into being in a sudden, explosive, and cataclysmic way. Yet, when you ask some highly intelligent people, *"What was that?"* they will claim, *"Nothing! It just happened."* With this illustration in mind, consider the following question posed by the Christian philosopher, William Lane Craig:

> "If there is obviously a cause for a little bang, doesn't it also make sense that there would be a Cause for a Big Bang?"[23]

2. THE UNIVERSE POPPED INTO EXISTENCE OUT OF NOTHING.

If science has now firmly established that the universe had a beginning, this begs the question, "What caused it to suddenly spring into existence?" Is it more plausible to believe that the universe was caused (as the Bible has stated all along) or uncaused? If we are to base our conclusions on the available evidence, common sense, logic, and human experience, one thing is abundantly clear: Things don't just pop into existence, uncreated, uncaused, out of nothing.

Ravi Zacharias tells the story of a conversation he had with a group of prestigious scientists and scholars about the origin of the universe. "If the Big Bang were indeed where it all began," he asked them, "what preceded the Big Bang?" Their answer, which he had anticipated, was that the universe was shrunk down to a singularity. "But isn't it correct," he pursued, "that a singularity as defined by science is a point at which all the laws of physics break down?" "That is correct," was the answer from this group. "Then, technically, your starting point is not scientific either," said Zacharias. Later, recalling their reaction to his comment, he writes, "There was silence, and their expressions betrayed the scurrying mental searches for an escape hatch."[24] Robert Jastrow, the founder-director of NASA's Goddard Institute of Space Studies, put it this way:

A sound explanation may exist for the explosive birth of our universe; but if it does, a scientist's pursuit of the past ends in the moment of creation... The scientist's quest for answers for the origin of the universe ends like a bad dream. In it, he has scaled the mountains of ignorance; he is about to conquer the highest peak; as he pulls himself over the final rock, he is greeted by a band of theologians who have been sitting there for centuries.[25]

3. THE UNIVERSE HAS A CREATOR.

The first sentence in the Bible is, "In the beginning God created the heavens and the earth."[26] This explanation of how the universe began is not only backed up by the recent scientific discoveries mentioned above, but simply makes the most sense and requires significantly less faith than the idea that, "In the beginning, Nothing went boom and then there was Everything." In his book entitled *The Case for a Creator,* Lee Strobel writes the following:

"In arguing for the existence of God, thirteenth-century Christian philosopher Thomas Aquinas always presupposed Aristotle's view that the universe is eternal. On the basis of that difficult assumption, he then sought to prove that God exists. Why did he take this approach? Because, Aquinas said, if he were to start with the premise that the universe had a beginning, then his task would be too easy!

Obviously, if there was a beginning, something had to bring the universe into existence. But now, modern astrophysics and astronomy have dropped into the lap of Christians precisely the premise that, according to Aquinas, makes God's existence virtually undeniable. Given that whatever begins to exist has a cause and that the universe began to exist, there must be some sort of transcendent cause for the origin of the universe."[27]

**If everything that has a beginning in our world came from something,
why in the world should we believe that the universe came from nothing?**

The Bible puts it this way:

"...Every house is built by someone, but God is the builder of everything."
(Hebrews 3:4)

"By faith we understand that the universe was formed at God's command, so that what is seen was not made out of what was visible."
(Hebrews 11:3)

"...God made the earth by his power; he founded the world by his wisdom and stretched out the heavens by his understanding."
(Jeremiah 10:12)

"If everything has a cause then what caused God?"

This is a good question because the answers can tell us a lot about God!

Consider the following descriptions of God in the Bible:

"Before the mountains were born or you brought forth the whole world, from everlasting to everlasting you are God."
(Psalm 90:2)

"God is spirit, and his worshipers must worship in the spirit and in truth."
(John 4:24)

" 'Am I only a God nearby,' declares the LORD, 'and not a God far away? Who can hide in secret places so that I cannot see them?' declares the LORD. 'Do not I fill heaven and earth?' declares the Lord."
(Jeremiah 23:23-24)

"...who is able to build a temple for him (God), since the heavens, even the highest heavens, cannot contain him?"
(2 Chronicles 2:6)

"But you remain the same, and your years will never end."
(Psalm 102:27)

"But do not forget this one thing, dear friends: With the Lord a day is like a thousand years, and a thousand years are like a day."
(2 Peter 3:8)

"'I am the Alpha and the Omega,' says the Lord God, 'who is, and who was, and who is to come, the Almighty.'"
(Revelation 1:8)

These verses tell us that God is eternal, unchanging, uncreated, and powerful. God is everywhere at the same time. He is Spirit. He is timeless. He is over and above the universe. He fills heaven and earth with His presence. He is always near. He has no beginning and no end. He is uncaused.

Thus, the clear biblical answer to the question "Where did God come from?" is "God has always been." To some, this answer is simply not satisfying. However, it is important to point out that while the idea of an eternal, uncaused, infinite God is certainly not easy to grasp, it is even more mystifying and mind-boggling to consider how our universe got here without a First Cause. For example, consider the problem philosophers call *infinite regression*. Simply stated, some ancient cultures taught that the earth was held up by a giant turtle. When an inquisitive child would ask, "What is holding up the turtle?" The parent would answer, "Another turtle." Invariably, the child would respond, "Well, what is holding up that turtle?" The answer "Another turtle" would be the same until the parent finally declared, "Look, it's turtles all the way down!" (You may remember that Dr. Seuss' book *Yertle the Turtle* picked up on this theme). In philosophical terms, the idea that "it's turtles all the way down" is called *infinite regression*. The turtle story is humorous to us because our minds immediately recognize that when seeking the cause behind an effect, infinite regression is no answer at all. When we are stopped by a long freight train and see a long chain of railroad boxcars, we intuitively know that there is an engine somewhere causing the boxcars to move, even though we may not be able to see it.

As we have seen, when it comes to the question, "How did the universe get here?" we only have a limited amount of options.

1. **The universe is eternal.**
2. **The universe is uncaused.**
3. **The universe is caused by something or someone.**

The first two options are unsupported by modern science. However, it is equally unhelpful to hold the position that the cause of the universe also had a cause. For example, those who do not believe in God may, instead, believe that the universe was caused by a quantum fluctuation, which must have been caused by something else, which must have been caused by something else, and on and on. Or, consider the Mormon belief that God is not eternal, thus He must have been caused to exist by another God, who must have been caused by, yet, another God... In other words, "It's turtles all the way down." The consensus among modern scientists is that the universe, matter, space, and time had a beginning and came into existence with a Big Bang. If this is true, does it not make sense then that the Cause of matter, space, and time must be immaterial, space-less, timeless, eternal, and uncaused? The thirteenth-century Italian theologian, Thomas Aquinas (1225-1274) summed it up this way:

- Everything that is caused is caused by something else.
- An infinite regress of causation is impossible.
- Therefore, there must be an uncaused cause of all caused things.

- This causer is what we call God.[28]

"Only things that had a beginning—like our universe—need a beginner. God had no beginning, so God did not need to be made."[29]

CHAPTER 4

Is There
an Intelligent Designer?

EVERY COMPLEX DESIGN
THAT SERVES A PURPOSE
HAS AN INTELLIGENT DESIGNER.

"The most miraculous thing is happening.
The physicists are getting down to the nitty gritty...
and the last thing they ever expected to be happening
is happening. God is showing through."

~ John Updike

1. Imagine that you are hiking in an area of the world that you believe no other person has ever been. As you are hiking, you see one rock balancing on another. Would you now suspect that someone had been there before you? Why or why not?

2. If you were hiking in the same area and saw several rocks on top of each other, largest at the bottom and smallest at the top, would you suspect that someone had been there before you? Why or why not?

3. If you were hiking and saw Mount Rushmore would you suspect that someone had been there before you? Why or why not?

Nature is somewhat predictable. We intuitively know that wind, rain, and snow did not create the faces of the four U.S. presidents on Mount Rushmore. The design is far too complex. It is obvious that an intelligent designer and a talented artist created this.

CONSIDER OUR UNIVERSE

From the outer regions of space to the microscopic world of atoms and molecules, our universe displays an astonishing level of complex design, purpose, beauty, order, and arrangement. In fact, there has never been a time in history when there has been a greater abundance of scientific evidence pointing to the existence of an Intelligent Designer of our universe. For example, let us turn our attention to a phenomenon that scientists now call the "anthropic principle." The term (derived from the Greek word *anthropos* for "man") was first introduced in 1974 by the Cambridge physicist Brandon Carter to express the idea that, from the beginning of its existence, the universe appears to have possessed just the right qualities for intelligent life to exist on planet earth. Since then, modern scientists have been astounded to discover one example after another that the universe just happened to spring into existence fully loaded with just the right delicate balance of physical laws, parameters, and cosmological constants to make life on earth possible.

Here are some examples of the complexity of our universe:

a) If our universe had not expanded at just the right speed at the moment of origin, life on earth would not have been possible. The famed astrophysicist Stephen Hawking has calculated that if the rate of the universe's expansion one second after the Big Bang had been smaller by even one part in a hundred thousand million million, the universe would have collapsed into a fireball.[30]

b) If the precise amount of matter were not produced at the moment of origin, the universe would have never formed.

c) If electrical, gravitational, electromagnetic, or nuclear forces in our universe were slightly stronger or weaker, life on earth would not be possible.

d) If planet earth were any closer to the sun, it would be too hot for life to exist on earth. If it were any farther away, it would be too cold for life to exist on earth. The distance happens to be just right!

e) If the size, composition, location, and orbit of the sun, earth, or moon were not just what they are, life on earth would not be possible.[31]

f) If the surface temperature of the sun was slightly higher or lower, life on earth would not be possible.

g) If the earth rotated around the sun at any other speed or diameter, life on earth would not be possible.

h) If the delicate ozone layer did not exist to filter out the sun's harmful ultraviolet rays—life on earth would not be possible. If the ozone level were smaller, there would be too much UV radiation for adequate plant growth. If the level were greater, there would be too little UV radiation for sufficient plant growth.

i) If the moon were any closer to earth, ocean tides would cover the highest mountains. If it were any bigger and in the same place, the tides would be too strong and life on earth would not be possible.

j) If the thickness of the earth's crust were slightly different, life on earth would not be possible.

k) If our planet did not have an abundant supply of carbon, oxygen, nitrogen, hydrogen, phosphorus, and calcium, life would not be possible. No other planet has been found to have all these crucial elements to sustain life.

l) If our planet were not covered with 4/5ths water which evaporates, gives us rain, and regulates temperature, life would not be possible.

m) If the process of atmospheric evaporation were not finely and precisely balanced, life on earth would not be possible.

n) If the range of temperature, humidity, pressure, or acidity in our atmosphere were any different, life on earth would not be possible.

o) If the severity of volcanic or seismic activity on earth were slightly greater or lesser, life on earth would not be possible.

p) If the speed of light constant, the electromagnetic fine structure constant, or the gravitational constant were slightly different, life on earth would not be possible. Dr. Patrick Glynn has observed, "All the seemingly arbitrary and unrelated constants in physics have one strange thing in common—these are precisely the values you need if you want to have a universe capable of producing life."[32] Michael A. Corey adds; "The fundamental laws and constants of nature did not gradually evolve into their present life-supporting character through a process of natural selection, as is widely believed. Instead, they spontaneously came into existence with the origin of the universe itself, perfectly calibrated and ready for action... Despite the infinity of possible errors, the universe repeatedly chose the 'correct' value each time it had to do so as far as our own existence is concerned. Mathematicians tell us that the probability for this happening is zero. Yet we are here."[33]

q) If the cosmological constant—the energy density of empty space —which is part of Einstein's equation for General Relativity, did not defy the astronomical odds of being precisely the right value, a life-bearing universe would not exist. Dr. Robin Collins, one of the most informed voices on the anthropic principle has stated, "The unexpected, counterintuitive, and stunningly precise setting of the cosmological constant is widely regarded as the single greatest problem facing physics and cosmology today... The fine-tuning (of the cosmological constant) has conservatively been estimated to be at least one part in a hundred million billion billion billion billion. That would be a ten followed by fifty-three zeroes. That's inconceivably precise... In my opinion, if the cosmological constant were the only example of fine tuning, and if there were no natural explanation for it, then this would be sufficient by itself to strongly establish design."[34]

You can see that we have a most fortunate planet. How do we explain these cosmic coincidences that make life possible? Does the complexity and fine-tuning of the universe point to an Intelligent Designer? John Lennox, Professor of Mathematics at the University of Oxford and Adjunct Lecturer at the Oxford Centre for Christian Apologetics said the following: "Life wouldn't have been possible if God hadn't of got the mathematics right!"

Many of today's leading scientists are acknowledging that apart from the deliberate workings of an Intelligent Designer, modern science has absolutely no adequate explanation for the billions of independent cosmic factors that happen to be "just right" for humans to exist. The evidence strongly suggests that all the physics and all the right conditions to sustain life had been carefully thought out before the beginning of time.

Have you ever wondered why the universe is so friendly toward life? Don't these astonishing observations cry out for an explanation? Where do these observations lead us? Could not all this fine tuning of the universe point to a Fine Tuner?

Michael A. Corey, in his book *The God Hypothesis*, presents the following analysis:

The entire universe does indeed 'cater' to the needs of humanity after all, insofar as it is permeated with the very same structural specifications that are necessary for human existence... These cosmic 'coincidences' between distant branches of physics are so compelling, in fact, that many scientists are actually coming forward and admitting that 'something must be going on behind the scenes.' Physicist Freeman Dyson said this, "As we look out into the universe and identify the many accidents of physics and astronomy that have worked together to our benefit, it almost seems as if the universe must in some sense have known that we were coming." [35]

Sir Roger Penrose calculated that the mathematical probability of our universe "just popping out of nowhere" with the mind-boggling degree of fine-tuning that enables us to exist to be 10 to the 10^{123}—a number that is so vast that it could not be written on a piece of paper the size of the entire visible universe! [36] The eminent British astrophysicist, Sir Fred Hoyle once commented, "A common sense interpretation of the facts suggests that a superintellect has monkeyed with physics, as well as chemistry and biology, and that there are no blind forces worth speaking about in nature." [37] Responding to this, Harvard professor of astronomy Owen Gingerich (senior astronomer at the Smithsonian Astrophysical Observatory) added, "Fred Hoyle and I differ on lots of questions, but on this we agree: a common sense and satisfying interpretation of our world suggests the designing hand of a super intelligence." [38] The evidence that our universe is "fine-tuned for life" is extremely compelling. For example, it would be weird enough to randomly find a concert harp on another planet, but if all of the 46 strings on the harp were perfectly in tune it would seem that even the most skeptical astronaut would begin to wonder if the harp had been placed there by an intelligent being. This example actually pales in comparison when considering our universe as the following analogy from Robin Collins points out:

"Suppose astronauts landed on Mars and found an enclosed biosphere, sort of like the domed structure that was built in Arizona a few years ago. At the control panel they find that all the dials for its environment are set just right for life. The oxygen ratio is perfect; the temperature is seventy degrees; the humidity is fifty percent; there's a system for replenishing the air; there are systems for producing food, generating energy, and disposing of wastes. Each dial has a huge range of possible settings, and you can see if you were to adjust one or more of them just a little bit, the environment would go out of whack and life would be impossible. Do you know what the headline would be in the newspaper the next day? It would say: EXTRATERRESTRIAL LIFE EXISTS. We would conclude that this biosphere was not there by accident. Volcanoes didn't erupt and spew out the right compounds that just happened to assemble themselves into the biosphere. Some intelligent being had intentionally and carefully designed and prepared it to support living creatures. And that's an analogy for our universe."[39]

Dr. Collins also acknowledges that the theological implications of the fine-tuning of our universe are profound, saying, "the facts concerning the universe's remarkable 'just-so' conditions are widely regarded as by far the most persuasive current argument for the existence of God."[40]

The Bible says:

"The heavens declare the glory of God; the skies proclaim the work of his hands. Day after day they pour forth speech; night after night they reveal knowledge. They have no speech, no words; no sound is heard from them. Yet their voice goes out into all the earth, their words to the end of the world."

(Psalms 19:1-4)

"Lift up your eyes and look to the heavens: Who created all these? He who brings out the starry host one by one and calls them each by name. Because of his great power and mighty strength, not one of them is missing."

(Isaiah 40:26)

"When I consider your heavens, the work of your fingers, the moon and the stars, which you have set in place, what is

mankind that you are mindful of them, human beings that you care for them?"
(Psalms 8:3-4)

Thus far, we have only discussed the complexity and the purposeful design of our universe.

Consider the complexity, design, and the beauty of nature!

In one of his early writings, Charles Darwin noted, "The sight of the peacock feather makes me sick." Darwin was fully aware that his general theory of evolution could not explain the sheer beauty we find in nature. The Bible, on the other hand, tells us about a God who created trees that were "pleasing to the eye." (Genesis 2:9) If our universe simply popped out of nothing, how do we explain the aesthetic nature of our planet? Why are there such striking colors and magnificent designs on plants and animals? For that matter, why should there be colors in an accidental universe in the first place?

Equally difficult to explain (apart from an Intelligent Designer) are the countless examples of intricacy, complexity, and ingenuity found in the animal kingdom. Dr. Rubel Shelly writes the following:

> "One of my favorite examples of a case in nature of intelligent design involves an insect. The bombardier beetle squirts a lethal mixture of two chemicals into the face of its enemy. When the two chemicals mix, they explode. In order to store those two chemicals in its own body until needed for self-defense, a chemical inhibitor is there to make them harmless. At the instant the beetle squirts the stored liquid from its tail, an anti-inhibitor is added to make the mixture explosive again. The slightest alteration in the chemical balance involved here would result in a race of exploded beetles in only one generation. How reasonable is it to put this complex process down to a lucky roll of the dice as opposed to creative design? Since nature is not an intelligent being, and consequently has no sense of purpose,

there must be Somebody behind nature who designed and built these flamethrowers in beetles." [41]

Consider the complexity of our own bodies!

Carl Sagan wrote this about the brain:

> "The information content of the human brain expressed in bits is probably comparable to the total number of connections among neurons—about a hundred trillion. If written out in English, that information would fill some twenty million volumes. The equivalent of twenty million books is inside the heads of every one of us. The brain is a very big place in a very small space... The neurochemistry of the brain is astonishingly busy, the circuitry of a machine more wonderful than any devised by humans."

The renowned Oxford atheist, Richard Dawkins wrote this about the cell:

> "Each nucleus of every cell in the human body contains a digitally coded database larger, in information content, than all 30 volumes of the Encyclopedia Britannica put together." [42]

The fascinating thing about life is that it not only consists of matter and chemicals, but also information. Phillip E. Johnson points out, "a theory of life not only has to explain the origin of matter but also the origin of the information." [43] For example, suppose you were in a cave and you believed that you were the first human being ever in this part of the cave. As you were trudging through, you suddenly discover ancient pictographs painted all over the wall. Would you still believe that you were the first human that has ever entered this cave? Would it change things if you crawled even deeper into the cave and found etchings on the wall shaped exactly like English letters that mysteriously spelled out: "GO AWAY! THIS IS MY CAVE AND, FRANKLY, I WISH TO BE ALONE!?" Whenever we see written information, we intuitively assume that there is intelligence behind it. A message always comes from a messenger.

Lee Strobel makes an important point about this: Every

experience we have about information—whether it's computer code, hieroglyphic inscription, a book, or a cave painting—points toward intelligence. The same is true about the information inside every cell in every living creature."[44] In living systems, the guidance that is needed to assemble everything comes from DNA (deoxyribonucleic acid). Every cell of every plant and animal has to have a DNA molecule. These molecules are made up of four basic elements—adenine, guanine, cytosine, and thymine (commonly referred to by the letters A, G, C and T). As these four 'letters' are arranged in different sequences they provide a blueprint for the assembly of the proteins needed for an organism to survive. Scientists tell us that a single strand of DNA holds enough information to fill a 6,000 volume encyclopedia. There is, in fact, "no entity in the known universe that stores and processes more information, more efficiently than the DNA molecule."[45] In other words, that which is encoded on DNA is purely and simply written information. Think about how long it would take to spell out the phrase 'HAPPY BIRTHDAY' by randomly dropping *Scrabble* letters onto a table. With this in mind, is it really reasonable to believe that the massive amount of specific information imprinted on every strand of DNA just happens by accident? Stephen Meyer explains the importance of this matter:

> "This issue has caused all naturalistic accounts of the origin of life to break down, because it's *the* critical and foundational question. If you can't explain where the information comes from, you haven't explained life, because it's the information that makes the molecules into something that actually functions."[46]

Lee Strobel, in his book *The Case for the Creator* concludes the following:

> "What do we make of the fact that DNA stores far more information in a smaller space than the most advanced supercomputer on the planet? What else can generate information but intelligence?... The conclusion was compelling: an intelligent entity has quite literally spelled out evidence of his existence through the four

chemical letters in the genetic code. It's almost as if the Creator autographed every cell."[47]

Consider the eye!

Humans have been trying to build a better camera for more than 250 years. However, even the most complex and advanced camera can't even closely compare to our eyes. Our eyes have more than 100 million rods, six million cones, automatic focus, a light meter which always adjusts to its setting, and lens covers that keep the dust off. Our eyes can focus at various distances and can distinguish among seven million variations of color! Each human eye moves 100,000 times each day and handles 1.5 million simultaneous messages. If you scratch your eyelid, it heals itself. Doctors can't even explain why there is no scar tissue left. Of course, none of this would matter if our eyes were not precisely "wired" to millions of nerve cells in the brain.[48]

Paul Davies, in his book entitled *Superforce* concludes the following:

> If nature is so 'clever' it can exploit mechanisms that amaze us with their ingenuity, is that not persuasive evidence for the existence of intelligent design behind the physical universe? If the world's finest minds can unravel only with difficulty the deeper workings of nature, how could it be supposed that those workings are merely a mindless accident, a product of blind chance? ...If physics is the product of design, the universe must have a purpose, and the evidence of modern physics suggests strongly to me that the purpose includes us.

The Bible says:

"For you created my inmost being; you knit me together in my mother's womb. I praise you because I am fearfully and wonderfully made; your works are wonderful, I know that full well."

(Psalms 139:13-14)

A PARABLE [49]

Once upon a time there was a family of mice who had lived all their lives in a large piano. Every day in their little piano world they heard the beautiful music of the instrument, filling all the dark spaces with pleasant sound and harmony. At first the mice were impressed by it. They drew comfort and wonder from the thought that there was Someone who made the music—invisible to them—yet close to them. They loved to think of the Great Player whom they could not see.

Then one day a daring young mouse named Charlie climbed up part of the piano and returned very thoughtful. He had discovered how the music was made. In fact, Charlie was a little disturbed by what he had discovered. Wires were the secret! Tightly stretched wires of graduated lengths which trembled and vibrated. He carefully and thoughtfully wrote a book about his discovery and called it *"The Origin of Music."* At first, Charlie's theory was met with resistance. But eventually, it became the predominate view of where the music was coming from. The mice had to revise all their old, outdated beliefs. None but the most naïve and conservative mice could any longer believe in the "Mysterious Unseen Player."

The really cool mice designed "Charlie" stickers and wore them with pride to show the other mice that they were not narrow-minded.

Later, other explorers carried the explanation further. Hammers were now the secret—numbers of hammers dancing and leaping on the wires. This was a more complicated theory, but it all went to show that they lived in a purely mechanical and mathematical world.

The Unseen Player came to be thought of as a myth.

All the while, the Pianist continued to play.

Silly mice.

CHAPTER 5

Does God Exist?

OBJECTIVE MORAL VALUES CAN EXIST ONLY IF GOD EXISTS OBJECTIVE MORAL VALUES DO EXIST THEREFORE, GOD MUST EXIST

Have you ever wondered why we feel a strange gnawing inside when we have done something wrong? Why do we experience a vague sense of emptiness when we violate our conscience and a warm sense of peace when we obey it? Why is it that when we decide to simply 'do whatever we please,' eventually we encounter an indistinct, sinking, sour emotion in the pit of our being? In Carlo Collodi's famous children's novel *The Adventures of Pinocchio*, we are reminded that to be fully human (as opposed to a piece of wood) is to possess a conscience. What is this inner voice of moral obligation? Where does it come from? In this chapter, we will explore these important questions.

In June of 2000, President Bill Clinton stood in the East Room of the White House and declared to the world that the "most important, wondrous map ever produced by humankind" had been assembled. He went on to say in this momentous announcement that "today, we are learning the language in which God created life. We are gaining ever more awe for the complexity, the beauty, and the wonder of God's most divine and sacred gift."[50] This "map" and "language" to which President Clinton was referring was the working draft of the human genome, the hereditary code of life. This "map" would help us to understand the genetic makeup of the human species and the hereditary information encoded on DNA. Standing beside the President on this historic occasion was Dr. Francis Collins, the leader of the International Human Genome Project, whose research team had labored for more than a decade to decipher this code and reveal the DNA sequence. Dr. Collins says in his book *The Language of God* that "this newly revealed text was 3 billion letters long, and written in a strange and cryptographic four-letter code. Such is the amazing complexity of the information carried within each cell of the human body, that a live reading of that code at a rate of one letter per second would take thirty-one years, even if reading continued day and night."[51]

This astonishing scientific discovery caused many to contemplate the following questions: What (or Who) is responsible for all this information in our DNA? What (or Who) designed this "map" and wrote this "language" that reveals the instruction book of life? Dr. Collins, an avowed atheist in his younger days, who later became one of the world's leading geneticists and the head of one of history's greatest scientific achievements, says the answer to these intriguing questions is none other than God.

Excuse me? A rigorously trained, modern-day, world-leading scientist who believes in God! Yes, it's true. In fact, Dr. Collins claimed that "for me the experience of sequencing the human genome, and uncovering this most remarkable of all texts, was both a stunning scientific achievement and an occasion of worship."[52]

What happened here? What caused a sincere, brilliant, atheistic scientist to adopt a firm belief in God—the God of the Bible, no less? Dr. Collins writes the following about his conversion:

My most awkward moment came when an older woman, suffering daily from severe untreatable angina, asked me what I believed. It was a fair question; we had discussed many other important issues of life and death, and she had shared her own strong Christian beliefs with me. I felt my face flush as I stammered out the words, "I'm not really sure." Her obvious surprise brought into sharp relief a predicament that I had been running away from for nearly all of my twenty-six years: I had never really considered the evidence for and against belief. That moment haunted me for several days. Did I not consider myself a scientist? Does a scientist draw conclusions without considering the data? Could there be a more important question in all of human existence than, "Is there a God?" And yet there I found myself, with a combination of willful blindness and something that could only be properly described as arrogance, having avoided any serious consideration that God might be a real possibility. Suddenly all my arguments seemed very thin, and I had the sensation that the ice under my feet was cracking... I determined to have a look at the facts, no matter what the outcome.[53]

In the process of "looking at the facts," Dr. Collins began conducting a personal survey of the major religions of the world. During this time, a neighbor suggested he read a book by C. S. Lewis titled *Mere Christianity.* He agreed and, like countless others, found Lewis' arguments for the existence of God extremely compelling and joltingly convincing. Collins writes, "The argument that most caught my attention, and most rocked my ideas about science and spirit down to their foundation, was right there in the title of Book One: 'Right and Wrong as a Clue to the Meaning of the Universe.'"[54]

What was it about C.S. Lewis' famous "Moral Law" argument for God's existence that was so captivating to one of the world's leading scientific minds? For the rest of this chapter, we will consider this question and Lewis' argument closely.

How do we decide who is right and who is wrong when it comes to morality?

When World War II was over, some of the war criminals were brought to trial. Many of them were asked, *"How could you kill so many innocent people?"* Some answered, *"I was just obeying the commands of my leaders and following the laws of my country."* The judges rightly asked, *"But, is there not a law that is **bigger and above** national laws? Isn't there a universally recognized law of morality that we all must live by?"*

If a law exists that is bigger and above national laws, human feelings, and personal opinions, then who created this universal moral law?

C. S. Lewis and many others argue that this law must come from someone who is bigger and above nations and humans. In other words, this law must come from God.

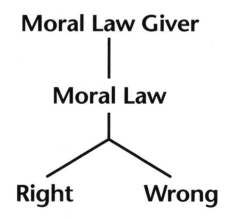

If there is no Moral Law Giver who transcends national laws, human feelings, and personal opinions, then there can be no objective moral law. Many atheistic philosophers affirm this. Jean-Paul Sartre (1905-1980) admits that this is the atheist's dilemma. This French existentialist philosopher remarked,

"…everything is indeed permitted if God does not exist, and man is in consequence forlorn, for he cannot find anything to depend upon either within or outside himself… Nor on the other hand if God does not exist, are we provided with any values or commands that could legitimize our behavior." [55]

Charles Darwin also acknowledged this. In his autobiography, Darwin admitted,

"A man who has no assured and ever present belief in the existence of a personal God or of a future existence with retribution and reward, can have for his rule of life, as far as I can see, only to follow those impulses and instincts which are the strongest or which seem to him the best ones." [56]

In the classic Russian novel *The Brothers Karamazov*, Fyodor Dostoyevsky (1821-81) wrote, "If God does not exist, everything is permissible." These writers recognized that the moment we take God out of the picture—right and wrong, good and evil go with him. In the process, we lose the right to say that anything is absolutely wrong or evil. Trying to decide who is right or wrong without the standard of an objective moral law is like trying to decide whose imaginary friend is more attractive. When God is no longer in the picture, terms like *morality, good, evil*, and *truth* can only be defined by conflicting human opinions, personal feelings or personal tastes. If morality is based solely on human opinion or personal feelings, we are left wondering, *Whose opinion or feelings should we choose to follow?* If nature is the author of the moral law, we are left asking, "Whose nature do we decide to follow?"

Of course, there are some objections to the moral law argument for the existence of God.

Some people say… *"This universal moral law came from thousands and thousands of years of social human evolution."*

Why does this not make sense?

Here are reasons why the idea of an evolution of morality does not make sense:

1. Evolution can't provide any adequate reasons for the existence of our conscience. If we are simply the product of chance mutation and a random collision of atoms, how do we explain this "voice of God in our soul?"[57] Ravi Zacharias writes, "Not one proponent of evolutionary ethics has explained how an impersonal, amoral first cause through a non-moral process can produce a moral basis of life."[58]

2. If morality is evolving, then society's morals should be getting better. Having just ended the bloodiest century in human history, it would be difficult to prove that we are progressing in the area of ethics and morality.

3. Evolutionary ethics can't explain why sometimes strong, healthy people will sacrifice their lives to save a weaker, unhealthy individual. C. S. Lewis provides us with a helpful illustration here. He asks us to imagine that you are walking down the road and suddenly hear a cry for help from someone in danger. At that moment, two competing instincts emerge within us: 1) A desire to help the person 2) A desire to avoid danger and run away. Suddenly, a third feeling enters into the picture that tells you that "you ought to follow the impulse to help, and suppress the impulse to run away." Where did this third impulse come from? Doesn't this go directly against evolution's directive of self preservation? Lewis writes,

   > "...at those moments when we are most conscious of the Moral Law, it usually seems to be telling us to side with the weaker of the two impulses. You probably *want* to be safe much more than you want to help the man who is drowning: but the Moral Law tells you to help him all the same."[59]

4. Can the Moral Law simply be attributed to social convention?

Here again, Lewis comes to our aid and gives two examples to help us distinguish what a social convention is and what it is not. British motorists drive on the left side of the road. Americans drive on the right side. This is an example of a social convention. There is no universal right or wrong on this matter. Mathematics, however, must be placed into a different category. The law of mathematics is objective and universal. In other words, even if the entire population of a particular country unanimously decided that $1 + 1 = 3$, they would still be entirely wrong based on a higher law, a real truth, which stands over and above this national decision. Most people will admit that the Moral Law clearly falls into this category.

5. If society is the author of the universal moral law, why do we admire social reformers? People like Martin Luther King Jr. inspire us because they have taken a stand against the established national laws of society. Social reformers do not base their idea of morality on the standard of right and wrong embraced by society. We respect these people because they appeal to a higher standard, which towers above established social conventions.

What is the relevance of the moral law argument?

Undoubtedly, the most famous exposition on the Moral Law argument for the existence of God comes from the first thirty-four pages of C. S. Lewis' *Mere Christianity.*

C. S. Lewis (1898-1963) entitled the first chapter of this classic book:

"Right and Wrong as a Clue of the Meaning of the Universe." In it, he reminds us that when people argue, they invariably appeal to a universal standard of behavior that everyone intuitively knows about. Quarrelling means "trying to show that the other man is in the wrong. And there would be no sense in trying to do that unless you and he had some sort of agreement as to what Right and Wrong are."

Lewis writes,

"The moment you say one set of moral ideas can be better than another, you are, in fact, measuring them both by a standard, saying that one of them conforms to that standard more nearly than the other... You are, in fact, comparing them both with some Real Morality, admitting that there is such a thing as a real Right, independent of what people think, and that some people's ideas get nearer to that real Right than others." [60]

This universal standard of behavior, which "we did not invent and which we know we ought to obey," is very much like other laws in our universe (such as the law of gravity) in that everyone is governed by it. However, as Lewis adds, there are several unique features about the moral law:

1) Humans can freely choose either to obey or disobey this law.

2) Although this law urges us to do right, we all break it at some point or another.

3) When we break this law, we feel uncomfortable and a sense of guilt.

Lewis points out that it would be near impossible to know that this law existed unless you were an "insider." If an alien were studying human beings by simply watching us,

"...they would never get the slightest evidence that we had this moral law. How could he? For his observations would only show what we did, and the moral law is about what we ought to do... In other words, when you are dealing with humans, something else comes in above and beyond the actual facts. You have the facts (how men do behave) and you also have something else (how they ought to behave)." [61]

4) This law suggests that we are not on our own and that "somebody or something wants me to behave in a certain way."

5) This Moral Law can serve as a clue to understanding what the Moral Law Giver is like. Lewis suggests that we can learn the following things about God by considering this law:

A. God is a moral being

"You find out more about God from the Moral Law than from the universe in general just as you find out more about a man by listening to his conversation than by looking at a house he has built. Now, from this second bit of evidence we conclude that the Being behind the universe is intensely interested in right conduct—in fair play, unselfishness, courage, good faith, honesty and truthfulness. In that sense we should agree with the account given by Christianity and some other religions, that God is 'good.'" [62]

B. God does not take morality lightly

Lewis goes on to say that "if God is like the Moral Law, then He is not soft." We know this because the Moral Law is as "hard as nails" in that it "tells you to do the straight thing and it does not seem to care how painful, or dangerous, or difficult it is to do." [63]

In summary, Lewis plants an uncomfortable and sobering thought. First of all, we intuitively know what we ought and ought not to do. Second, at times, we all choose to do what we ought not to do, thus we all break this Moral Law. Third, the Creator of the Universe does not take this lightly. If these disconcerting ideas are true then it may occur to us... "Hey, wait a minute... I may be in serious trouble!" C. S. Lewis concludes the following about the implications of this objective moral law:

...we know that if there does exist an absolute goodness it must hate most of what we do. This is the terrible fix we are in. If the universe is not governed by an absolute goodness, then all our efforts are in the long run hopeless. But if it is, then we are making ourselves enemies to that goodness every day, and are not in the least likely to do any better tomorrow, and so our case is hopeless again. We cannot do without it, and we cannot do with it. God is the only comfort, He is also the supreme terror: the thing we most need and the thing we most want to hide from. He is our only possible ally, and we have made ourselves His enemies... It is after you have realized that there is a real Moral Law, and a Power behind the law, and that you have broken that law and put yourself wrong with that Power—it is after all this, and not a moment sooner, that Christianity begins to talk. When you know you are sick, you will listen to the doctor. When you have realized that our position is nearly desperate you will begin to understand what the Christians are talking about... They tell you how the demands of this law, which you and I cannot meet, have been met on our behalf, how God Himself becomes a man to save man from the disapproval of God.[64]

The Bible says:

"You see, at just the right time, when we were still powerless, Christ died for the ungodly. Very rarely will anyone die for a righteous man, though for a good person someone might possibly dare to die. But God demonstrates his own love for us in this: While we were still sinners, Christ died for us. Since we have now been justified by his blood, how much more shall we be saved from God's wrath through him! For if, when we were God's enemies, we were reconciled to him through the death of his Son, how much more, having been reconciled, shall we be saved through his life! Not only is this so, but we also boast in God through our Lord Jesus Christ, through whom we have now received reconciliation."

(Romans 5:6-11)

QUESTIONS FOR DARWIN

by Russ Whitten

So you think you know the answer
about how we came to be?

Do you think our ancestors were really chimpanzees?

Did something really come from nothing
complete with complexity?

Is it human opinion that defines morality?

If everything in this world has a cause
what caused the universe?

If all art has an artist
do you believe nature's art came first?

Did mind create matter or did matter create mind?

Is random chance the father of life,
complex order and design?

Who is responsible for the information in my DNA?

Charles Darwin, tell me, where's the hope
at the end of your day?

CHAPTER 6

Is the Bible Really the Word of God?

Christians believe that God has communicated with us through the Bible. How do we judge whether this is true or not? What evidence is there that the Bible is trustworthy, reliable, and any different than other sacred religious books?

In the next two chapters, we will look at the following two questions:

1. **If God wrote a book, what sort of qualities would you expect from it?**
2. **Does the Bible display the qualities and characteristics we would expect if it were from God?**

I. If God wrote a book, we would expect that He would tell us that He wrote it.

In the Old Testament alone, there are over 3,800 claims that the Scriptures are ultimately from God. In fact, the Bible claims that it comes from the very breath of God.

> "All Scripture is God-breathed and is useful for teaching, rebuking, correcting and training in righteousness, so that the servant of God may be thoroughly equipped for every good work." (2 Timothy 3:16-17)

The Bible claims that God inspired people to write exactly what He wanted them to write.

> "Above all, you must understand that no prophecy of Scripture came about by the prophet's own interpretation of things. For prophecy never had its origin in the human will, but prophets,

though human, spoke from God as they were carried along by the Holy Spirit." (2 Peter 1:20-21)

Jesus described the Scriptures as the "word that comes from the mouth of God." (Matthew 4:4)

II. If God wrote a book, we would expect that it would be a popular book.

A. No book in the world even begins to approach the Bible in terms of circulation and popularity.

B. No other book has been translated more than the Bible.

C. As of September 2016, complete books of the Bible have been translated into 2,932 languages.[65]

D. The entire Bible has been published in 554 languages.

E. The entire New Testament has been published in more than 1,333 languages.

F. The Bible can now be read by more than 90 percent of the world population in their own language. According to the United Bible Societies: "We are less than a generation away from the Bible becoming the world's first universally translated book."[66]

G. The Bible is the best-selling book internationally year after year.

H. No book has ever had more influence on history, civilization, ethics, art, music, literature, architecture, philosophy, law, governments, politics, healthcare, education, humanitarian efforts, and even our calendar than the Bible.

I. There have been more books written about the Bible than any other book.

J. The Bible is the most scrutinized book ever written. This sets it apart from the Qur'an, which is never to be questioned or scrutinized according to Islam.

III. If God wrote a book, we would expect it to be timeless.

Think about history books, maps, scientific literature, and encyclopedias. These types of books are reprinted every few years and sometimes are outdated even before they come from the press. "Most men cannot even agree with their own writings after 10 years," Floyd McElveen suggests. "Try getting just 10 science textbooks spread over 20 or 30 years together, and compare them."[67] In contrast, the content and message of the Bible has always remained the same, yet it has never been considered outdated. The Bible speaks to every generation. Its universal message has given hope, peace, strength, meaning, and comfort to people from every nation and every generation for more than 2,000 years. Charles Dickens once commented that the Bible is "the very best book that ever was or ever will be known in the world."[68]

IV. If God wrote a book, we would expect that it would be understood by everyone.

The Bible appeals to every culture and every age. Young children can understand the simple stories of God's love and protection, while the most educated scholars are amazed at the Bible's profound depth and complexity. The Bible is "a pool in which a child may wade and an elephant can swim. It is both simple and profound. It is immediate and neverfailing."[69]

V. If God wrote a book, we would expect it to be perfectly coherent and consistent throughout.

The Bible is a collection of 66 books written by about 40 different people over a span of 1,600 years of human history. These writers were from different cultural, economic, geographical, and educational backgrounds. Some of the biblical writers were kings or political leaders. Some were warriors or military commanders. Others were priests, shepherds, or fishermen. Some were poor and others were quite rich. One was a former tax collector (a despised occupation in the first century), and another was a medical doctor. The Bible was written in three different languages—Hebrew, Greek, and Aramaic. It was written on three continents—Europe, Asia, and Africa. It contains many different styles and genres of literature. The writers worked independently from one another at different periods of history. In fact, many of the writers never met another biblical writer. The books, for the most part, were 66 independent compositions.

Yet, amazingly, when these books were collected and put into one volume, one complete and profoundly beautiful story emerged that displays a perfect harmony of unity, theme, focus, message, and teaching. Remarkably, when these books were combined, there were no contradictions. The Old and New Testaments present themselves as "two halves of a sentence: both are necessary before we can grasp the whole meaning."[70] British theologian J. I. Packer commented that the Bible has "an organic coherence that is simply stunning. Books written centuries apart seemed to have been designed for the express purpose of supplementing and illuminating each other... Truly, the inner unity of the Bible is miraculous: a sign and wonder challenging the unbelief of our skeptical age."[71]

Dr. Norman Geisler adds, "This incredible unity amidst such great diversity can best be accounted for by a God who stands outside of time and history and has weaved each of the pieces into one overall mosaic of truth and hope."[72]

VI. If God wrote a book, we would expect that it would change lives and society for the better.

The power of the Bible to change individual lives and society for the better is indisputable. Countless people have been changed for the better because they have read and followed the teachings in the Bible. This book has helped people find peace, courage, strength, comfort, and hope during the darkest of times. It has assisted people to be liberated from enslaving addictions. It has given people the courage to face death and the faith that there will be life even after we die. It was this book that inspired courageous leaders such as Martin Luther King, Jr. (1929-1968) to fight and even die for the cause of civil rights. It was this book that motivated the British politician William Wilberforce (1759-1833) to become a leader in the movement to abolish the slave trade.

Not too long ago, there was a highly publicized debate between a Christian minister and an atheistic philosopher. The atheist was trying to convince the audience that the Bible is just another book with no inherent "power" to change lives. The Christian speaker presented the following scenario to the philosopher. He asked, "What if you were driving and found yourself lost in a part of the city that was well known for being extremely dangerous and violent? As you make a wrong turn down a dark alley, all of a sudden, your car sputters and comes to a complete stop. You try desperately to get the car started again, but it just won't start. You quickly notice a gang of men slowly approaching the car. *Would it matter or not to you if you knew that these men were coming from a Bible study?"* After the laughter subsided, the philosopher conceded, "Yes, I have to admit that it would ease my fears if I knew that the gang of men was coming from a Bible study!"[73]

The American Bible Society once conducted an interesting experiment in Chicago. They chose a 5-block area in a district with one of the highest crime rates in the city and flooded it with copies of the Gospel of John. They included an invitation for anyone who wanted more reading material to send for a copy of the complete New Testament. They received many requests. The district police captain later reported that the crime rate in the area dropped dramatically in one month's time. The same experiment produced similar results in another area with a high crime rate.[74]

Even anti-Christian thinkers have been captivated by the inner beauty of the Bible. For example, Jean-Jacques Rousseau (1712-1778) once commented,

"I must confess to you that the majesty of the scriptures astonishes me… if it had been the invention of men, the inventors would be greater than the greatest heroes." [75]

John Bunyan, the author of the book *Pilgrims Progress*, once wrote this about the Bible:

"This book will keep you from sin, or sin will keep you from this book." [76]

"For the word of God is living and active. Sharper than any double-edged sword, it penetrates even to dividing soul and spirit, joints and marrow; it judges the thoughts and attitudes of the heart." (Hebrews 4:12)

VII. If God wrote a book, we would expect that it would be powerful.

The Bible makes the claim that it will never be destroyed:

"Heaven and earth will pass away, but my words will never pass away." (Mark 13:31)

"…All people are like grass, and all their glory is like the flowers of the field; the grass withers and the flowers fall, but the word of the Lord endures forever." (1 Peter 1:24-25)

Theodore Beza, the 16th-century Swiss theologian writes, "The Bible is an anvil that has broken many hammers." These words are proven true when we consider that many people, empires, and governments throughout the ages have tried to destroy, extinguish, suppress, and discredit the Bible, yet it survives and continues to flourish.

1) In 100 B. C., Antiochus IV (King of the Seleucid Empire who brutally persecuted the Jews) burned all the Scriptures he

could find and decreed death to all owners, yet, the Scriptures survived.

2) In A.D. 301-304, the Roman Emperor, Diocletian, burned thousands of copies of the Bible, commanded that all Bibles be destroyed, and decreed that any home with a Bible in it should be burned. In fact, he even built a monument over what he thought was the last surviving Bible. He then proudly proclaimed, *"The Christian name has been extinguished!"* The very next emperor, Constantine, made Christianity the state religion of Rome. Five hundred years after Diocletian's death, his grave (a huge mausoleum) became a church.

3) The Roman general and nephew of Constantine named Julian proclaimed that his book entitled *Refutation of the Christian Religion* would destroy the Bible forever. Have you ever heard of this book?

4) Voltaire, the great French Philosopher (1694-1778) once declared, "In 100 years, the Bible would be a forgotten and unknown book." A hundred years later, the Geneva Bible Society occupied his home. In 1778, Voltaire proudly boasted, "It took 12 men to start Christianity; one (referring to himself) will destroy it." Later, that year, he died.

5) The American political leader, Robert G. Ingersoll (1833-1899) once proclaimed, "In 15 years, I will have this book (the Bible) in the morgue." Fifteen years later, Robert Ingersoll was in the morgue.

6) Lew Wallace (1827-1905) who served as a writer, a Civil War general, a Governor of the territory of New Mexico and U.S. ambassador to Turkey was a known atheist. For two years, he studied at the leading libraries in Europe seeking information for his book that he believed would disprove the Bible and "forever destroy Christianity." While writing the second chapter of this book, he found himself on his knees praying

to Jesus. Because of the indisputable evidence, he could no longer deny that the Bible was the Word of God. Later, he wrote *Ben Hur* one of the greatest English novels ever written concerning the time of Christ.

7) During the 1950s, the Soviet Government (which outlawed owning or studying the Bible) built a majestic building in Kiev, Ukraine to house the Communist headquarters for that region. In 1994, I had the privilege of teaching the Bible to the entire freshman class in that building which then housed one of the first Christian universities in the former Soviet Union.

VIII. If God wrote a book, we would expect that it would be true.

If a book is really from God, we would expect it to be historically, scientifically, archeologically, philosophically, and morally accurate.

A. IS THE BIBLE HISTORICALLY ACCURATE?

About 150 years ago, it became popular to criticize the Bible because some people felt that it had historical mistakes in it, and some believed that eventually archaeology would prove that the Bible is not historically accurate. However, just the opposite happened. Modern archaeology has helped us realize that the Bible is historically accurate even in the smallest of details.[77] There have been thousands of archaeological discoveries in the past century that support every book of the Bible. Here are just a few examples:

Critics used to believe...

...that Moses could not have written any of the books of the Bible because they believed that writing did not exist that early in history...

but then...

...in 1902, archaeologists discovered the Code of Hammurabi which was written long before Moses was born.[78]

Critics used to believe...

...the Bible was wrong because they felt that King David was a legendary, mythical character. They pointed to the fact that there was no archeological evidence that King David was an actual historical figure...

but then...

...in 1994 archaeologists discovered an ancient stone slab in northern Galilee that was inscribed with the references to King David and the "House of David."

Critics used to believe...

...that the Bible was wrong because there was no evidence (outside of the Bible) that a group of people called the Hittites ever existed. The Hittite civilization is mentioned approximately forty times in the Old Testament, thus skeptics were convinced that this proved the Bible is a mythical creation of ancient Hebrew writers...

but then...

...in 1906, a German archaeologist named Hugo Winckler was excavating in Boghaz-Koi, Turkey and discovered the capital city of the ancient Hittite empire, the entire Hittite library and 10,000 clay tablets documenting the Hittite history. Scholars translated these writings and discovered that everything the Bible said about the Hittite empire was true.

Critics used to believe...

...that a King named Belshazzar never really existed, thus calling into question the historicity of the book of Daniel, which mentions this Babylonian king...

but then...

...in 1854, Henry Rawlinson discovered an inscription in Iraq that named Belshazzar as the oldest son and co-regent of King Nebonidus, who would often leave Belshazzar in charge of Babylon while he traveled. This discovery also helped to clarify Daniel

5:29, which states that Daniel was elevated to the "third highest ruler in the kingdom."

Critics used to believe...

...the book of Acts was not historically accurate. A man named Sir William Ramsay, who is well known to be one of the greatest historical scholars and archaeologists in history, decided to try to disprove the Bible as the inspired Word of God by showing that the book of Acts was not historically accurate...

but then...

...after 30 years of archaeological research in the Middle East, Ramsay came to the conclusion that "Luke is a historian of the first rank; not merely are his statements of fact trustworthy...this author should be placed along with the very greatest historians." He later wrote a book on the trustworthiness of the Bible based on his discoveries [79] and converted to Christianity. Sir Ramsay found no historical or geographical mistakes in the book of Acts. This is amazing when we realize that in the book of Acts, Luke mentions 32 countries, 54 cities, 9 Mediterranean islands and 95 people, and he did not get one wrong. Compare that with the *Encyclopedia Britannica*. The first year the *Encyclopedia Britannica* was published it contained so many mistakes regarding places in the United States that it had to be recalled.[80]

Critics used to believe...

...that the Old Testament simply could not be reliable because they felt that over a long period of time, the Old Testament writings would have been changed, altered, edited, or corrupted...

but then...

...in 1947, the Dead Sea Scrolls were discovered. These scrolls contained, among other writings, every book in the Old Testament (except Esther). Until the Dead Sea Scrolls were found, the earliest copy of the complete Old Testament was from A.D. 900. Scholars compared this copy with the Dead Sea Scrolls (produced around 1,000 years earlier) and found that the Old Testament had been handed down accurately through the centuries.

Archaeologists used to be puzzled...

...because a 1969 excavation of Gezer (the ancient city of Canaan located about 20 miles northwest of Jerusalem) revealed a thick layer of ash curiously containing Egyptian, Philistine, and Hebrew artifacts. This discovery seemed to suggest the unlikely possibility that all three cultures had been there at the same time.

but then...

...researchers looked in the Bible and found their explanation. First Kings 9:16-17 revealed that "Pharaoh king of Egypt had attacked and captured Gezer, and set it on fire...killed its Canaanite (Philistine) inhabitants, and then gave it as a wedding gift to his daughter, Solomon's wife. And Solomon (the Hebrew king) rebuilt Gezer..."

The prestigious Smithsonian Institution's Department of Anthropology has offered the following official statement pertaining to the historical reliability of the Old Testament:

> "...the historical books of the Old Testament, are as accurate historical documents as any that we have from antiquity and are in fact more accurate than many of the Egyptian, Mesopotamian, or Greek histories. These Biblical records can be and are used as are other ancient documents in archeological work."[81]

In other words, not only does archaeology confirm that the Bible is historically accurate, but professional archeologists actually use the Bible as a guide in their work. Compare the above statement about the Bible's historical reliability with, for example, the Smithsonian's official proclamation about the *Book of Mormon*:

> "The Smithsonian Institution has never used the Book of Mormon

in any way as a scientific guide. Smithsonian archeologists see no direct connection between the archeology of the New World and the subject matter of the book."[82]

The great Jewish archaeologist, Nelson Glueck (who is known to be one of the top three archaeologists in history) has stated the following:

"No archaeological discovery has ever contradicted a single, properly understood Biblical statement." [83]

B. IS THE BIBLE SCIENTIFICALLY ACCURATE?

The Bible was written centuries ago, and it has many verses in it that relate to science. One would expect that the lack of modern scientific knowledge of the writers would show through on this ancient document. But instead, there is an amazing treatment of science in the Bible that transcends human invention and the knowledge of the period in which it was produced.

Consider what the Bible does not say...

In 1862, an American adventurer and antiquities dealer named Edwin Smith purchased an ancient Egyptian medical book in Luxor. Ten years later, Egyptologist George Ebers purchased and helped translate it. It is now known as the *Papyrus Ebers*. It was written in Egypt about 1552 B.C. (around the time of Moses). In his book, *None of These Diseases,* Dr. S. I. McMillen writes, "Since Egypt occupied the dominant position in the ancient medical world, the Papyrus is of great importance as a record of the medical knowledge of that day."[84] When it was translated, it was really humorous as to what they believed. For example, the *Papyrus Ebers* provided the following medical advice...

> *"To prevent hair from turning gray, anoint it with the blood of a black calf which has been boiled in the fat of a rattlesnake."*

"To prevent balding, mix together the fat of a horse, a hippopotamus, a crocodile, a cat, a snake and an ibex. Then mix in the tooth of a donkey crushed in honey."

"Victims of poisonous snake bites are to be treated with 'magic water.' Water is considered 'magic' when it has been poured over an idol."

"Splinters are to be treated with a mixture of worm's blood and donkey dung."

"To stop bleeding, rub donkey dung on a cut."

"To remove wrinkles, split a toad in half and apply to wrinkled area."

The ancient Egyptians also believed that our planet was supported by five great pillars, that the earth was flat, that blood contained evil spirits and that there was spontaneous generation of life. Again, scholars have dated *Papyrus Ebers* back to the time of Moses. With this in mind, it is interesting to consider where Moses grew up and received his education. Acts 7:22 tells us, "Moses was educated in all the wisdom of the Egyptians..." Don't you think that we could expect to see some traces of scientific ignorance or medicinal errors shining through in the ancient writings of Moses? Yet, remarkably, we see no scientific mistakes. Not only is this true, but what we do find is that some of our "modern scientific discoveries" were recorded in the Bible the whole time. Consider the following examples:

What the Bible Said All Along	Scientific Discoveries
God told the Israelites to separate people who had infection and disease from the rest of the community (Leviticus 13).	In the 1500's, the Black Plague was killing many people in Europe. Then the people began following the Bible's teachings to separate those who had diseases. This practice helped to end the Black Plague.
God gave the Israelites many teachings about the washing of hands and clothing (Numbers 19:11-16).	The importance of washing to prevent the spread of germs was not recognized until 1865 by Joseph Lister.
God told the Israelites to let the land rest every seventh year (Leviticus 25:4).	Today, the practice of "letting the land rest" is known to be very important for the soil. This was not practiced, however, (except for the Israelites) until about 200 B.C. by the Romans.
God told the Israelites in Genesis 17:12 "every male among you who is eight days old must be circumcised . . ."	In 1935, doctors discovered that the best day for a surgical procedure on a newborn baby is on the 8th day because the blood is at the height of clotting on this day.
Isaiah 40:22 tells us the earth is round.	Most cultures before the 16th century believed that the earth was flat.
Job 26:7 tells us that "God hung the world on nothing."	Most ancient cultures believed that the world was held up by something.
Isaiah 43:16 and Psalm 8:6-8 talk about the "paths of the sea."	In 1855, Matthew Fountaine Maury, the "father of oceanography" discovered that there were natural currents and paths in the ocean.
God told Noah exactly how to design the ark in Genesis 6:15.	Navel engineers now know that this design is perfect for the rough seas.
Job 38:20 speaks about light moving from one place to another.	The fact that light moves was not known until Newton discovered the motion of light in the 1600s.

The prophet Jeremiah said that "no person can count all the stars" (Jeremiah 33:22).	At one time in history some people believed that we could count and even name all stars. Astronomers now understand that the stars are uncountable.
Ecclesiastes 1:6 describes global wind patterns.	Global wind patterns were not understood until the 1960s with the help of satellites.
Job 36:27-28, and Ecclesiastes 1:7 describes the water cycles.	This process was not understood by scientists until Perrault and Marriotte in the 1700s.

C. CONCLUSION:

In 1990, *Time* magazine asked the following question on its front cover: "How True Is the Bible?" The writer of this article concluded the following:

"After more than two centuries of facing the heaviest scientific guns that could be brought to bear, the Bible has survived—and is perhaps the better for the siege. Even on the critics' own terms —historical fact—the Scriptures seem more acceptable now than they did when the rationalists began the attack. Noting one example among many, New Testament Scholar Bruce Metzger observes that the Book of Acts was once accused of historical errors for details that have since been proved by archaeologists and historians to be correct." [85]

IX. If God wrote a book, we would expect it to display supernatural power.

Deuteronomy 18:21-22 says this:

"You may say to yourselves, 'How can we know when a message has not been spoken by the Lord?' If what a prophet proclaims in the name of the Lord does not take place or come true, that is a message the Lord has not spoken..."

According to this test, a person was to be considered a false prophet if his or her prophecies were not 100 percent correct 100 percent of the time. In other words, it would only take *one* false prophecy to reveal a false prophet. The same is true about a book. If a book claims that it is speaking for God and predicts that something will happen in the future, but the prediction is wrong, then you can know with certainty that the book is not from God.

The Bible contains numerous examples of predictive prophecy showing that God is the only possible author. The Bible has more than 1,000 prophecies in it about people, places, and events. No biblical prophecy has ever been proven false! Only the Bible is 100 percent correct in its prophecies. This fact sets the Bible far apart from every other book ever written.

HERE ARE SOME EXAMPLES:

Prophecy
The prophet Isaiah writing around 740-681 B.C. predicted that a leader named Cyrus would lead an army against the Babylonians and allow God's faithful people to return to Jerusalem and rebuild the temple. At the time of Isaiah's prophecy, the Assyrians, not the Babylonians, controlled Jerusalem and the temple was standing untouched. This prophecy is found in Isaiah 44:24-45.

Fulfillment
Jerusalem and the temple were destroyed in 586 B.C. by the nation of Babylon. In 537 B.C., Persia defeated Babylon. One hundred and fifty years after the prophecy, the Persian King Cyrus, a man who was not even born when Isaiah predicted this, victoriously led the Medo-Persian armies against the Babylonians and declared that the captives were free to return to Jerusalem and rebuild the temple.

Prophecy

In 586 B.C., the city of Tyre was considered one of the most powerful seaports in the world. At this time, the prophet Ezekiel predicted that Tyre would be destroyed by Babylon and other nations. He also predicted that the city would be flattened, reduced to a simple place to fish and that the city would never be rebuilt. These prophecies can be found in Ezekiel 26.

Fulfillment

That very year, Babylon destroyed part of the city of Tyre. Then, in 332 B.C., Alexander the Great destroyed the rest of the city and it was never rebuilt. Today, the place is just a flat rock where people fish.

In chapter 11, we will discuss the hundreds of prophecies in the Old Testament about the Messiah, which were fulfilled during the life of Jesus Christ.

There are many prophecies in the Bible about the end of the world, Jesus' return, judgment, heaven, and hell that have not yet been fulfilled. Since the Bible has proven itself to be correct 100 percent of the time in the prophecies that *have* been fulfilled, should we not think it wise to take seriously the prophecies that *have not yet* been fulfilled?

The offer of the gift of forgiveness of sins, an abundant life, and eternal life through Jesus Christ is the core message of the Bible. This good news sets the Bible apart from all other books!

CHAPTER 7

Can We Trust the Bible?

Have you ever wondered if the Bible is trustworthy and reliable? In this chapter, we will look at reasons to believe that we can trust and depend on the Bible. Let us begin by considering the trustworthiness of the New Testament.[86]

1) We have a great quantity of reliable, early copies of the New Testament books.

There are more than 5,300 ancient Greek manuscripts of the New Testament from close to the time the originals were written. Furthermore, these copies are from many different geographical areas. The New Testament scholar Bruce Metzger explains it this way:

> "In addition to the Greek manuscripts, we also have translations of the gospels in other languages at a relatively early time. For example, there are more than 8,000 ancient Latin copies of the New Testament. Even if we had no Greek manuscripts today, by piecing together the information from these translations we could actually reproduce the contents of the New Testament. In addition to that, even if we lost all the Greek manuscripts *and* the early translations we could still reproduce the contents of the New Testament from the multiplicity of quotations in commentaries, sermons, letters, and so forth of the early church fathers."[87]

Dr. Norman Geisler also points out: "The abundance of manuscript copies, about 24,970 manuscripts in all, makes it possible to reconstruct the original with virtually complete accuracy."[88] The oldest portion of the New Testament we have today is from the Gospel of John. It is called John Ryland's

Fragment (P52). Scholars have dated this portion of John's gospel to about A.D. 125 (which is only about thirty years after John wrote the original manuscript). The interesting thing about this scrap is that it was found in a community along the Nile River in Egypt, far from Ephesus where the gospel of John (the last of the four Gospels about Jesus) was written.

2) There is a remarkably small gap of time between the original New Testament writings and the oldest existing manuscript copies.

When trying to discern the trustworthiness of an ancient document, scholars will first consider two things: 1) The number of existing copies. 2) The time gap between the original writing of the document and the earliest existing copy. When it comes to the Bible, we find that it is by far the most documented work of ancient literature in the history of the world. Furthermore, the time gap between the originals and the earliest copies is remarkably small as shown on the following table.

Author & Book	Time Gap between the Original Writing and Earliest Existing Copy	Number of Existing Copies
Herodotus, *History*	ca. 1,350 yrs.	8
Thucydides, *History*	ca. 1,300 yrs.	8
Plato	ca. 1,300 yrs.	7
Demosthenes	ca.1,400 yrs.	200
Caesar, *Gallic Wars*	ca. 1,000 yrs.	10
Livy, *History of Rome*	ca. 400 yrs. ca. 1,000 yrs.	1 partial 19 copies
Tacitus, *Annals*	ca. 1,000 yrs.	20
Pliny Secundus, *Natural History*	ca. 750 yrs.	7
New Testament	fragment of a book: 30 yrs. books of the NT: 100 yrs. most of the NT: 150 yrs. complete NT: 225 yrs.	More than 5,366 Greek manuscripts 24,970 ancient manuscripts in all

Dr. Norman Geisler[89]

Floyd McElveen writes the following:

> "Even if someone deliberately or by accident emended or corrupted a manuscript, it would be corrected by the many other manuscripts available. To sum up; unless we want to throw a blanket over all of history and say that there is nothing knowable about the past, no history that can be trusted, no Grecian or Roman history, no Aristotle or Plato or Socrates, we had better not make any claims against the historicity and accuracy of the New Testament. The New Testament documents are far more numerous, older, demonstrably more accurate historically, and have been examined by a far greater battery of scholars, both friend and foe, than all the other ancient manuscripts put together. They have met the test impeccably!" [90]

"I'm disturbed by the fact that we do not have the originals and the copies are known to have mistakes in them!"

There are some minor variants in the biblical manuscripts. However...

- Such variants are relatively rare in the copied manuscripts and are mostly single letters or grammatical differences.

- In most cases, we know which variant is wrong from the context or the parallel passages.

- In no case do the variants call into question any core doctrine of the Christian faith.

- The variants actually vouch for the accuracy of the copying process, since the scribes who copied them knew that mistakes existed in the manuscripts, still they were duty-bound to copy exactly what the text said.

- The variants do not affect the message of the Bible. For example, one manuscript copy reads *"Holy, Holy is our God"* when most other texts read *"Holy, Holy, Holy is our God."*

- Most credible Bible translations note exactly where the manuscript variants are located and spell out which manuscripts contain alternate readings of a particular text. This should give us confidence that the translators have nothing to hide.

Yes, there are variants in the copies, but the multitude of manuscripts serves to cancel them out so that we can determine the correct reading.

3) The authors of the New Testament were in a position to report accurate historical information.

Matthew, John, and Peter were apostles (the original twelve disciples called by Jesus to carry the Christian message to the world) and eyewitnesses of the events they wrote about. Paul and James were later recognized as apostles because they had seen Jesus after he had been raised from the dead. Luke was Paul's travel companion and 'beloved physician' (Colossians 4:14). Papias, who wrote in about A.D. 125, affirmed that Mark had carefully and accurately recorded Peter's eyewitness observations. Irenaeus writing in about A.D. 180 confirmed the traditional authorship of the gospels. He wrote,

> "Matthew published his own Gospel among the Hebrews in their own tongue, when Peter and Paul were preaching the Gospel in Rome and founding the church there. After their departure, Mark, the disciple and interpreter of Peter, himself handed down to us in writing the substance of Peter's preaching. Luke, the follower of Paul, set down in a book the Gospel preached by his teacher. Then John, the disciple of the Lord, who also leaned on his breast, himself produced his Gospel while he was living at Ephesus in Asia."[91]

4) The New Testament was written during the lifetimes of eyewitnesses.

Norman Geisler reminds us, "The standard scholarly dating, even in very liberal circles, is still within the lifetimes of various eyewitnesses of the life of Jesus, including hostile eyewitnesses who would have served as a corrective if false teachings about Jesus were going around."[92] In other words, if the gospels were not true, all someone would have to do was to say, *"Hey, wait a minute! I was there and it didn't actually happen that way!"* The apostle Peter put it this way: "We did not follow cleverly invented stories when we told you about the power and coming of our Lord Jesus Christ, but we were eyewitnesses of his majesty" (2 Peter 1:16).

5) The New Testament writers would have wanted to preserve accurate history and were willing to die for it.

Toward the end of the first century, the apostles were dying out. Thus, it was extremely important to the New Testament writers to accurately preserve Jesus' teachings. Luke, for example, writes the following concerning his deep desire to record the story of Jesus truthfully, precisely, and carefully.

> "Many have undertaken to draw up an account of the things that have been fulfilled among us, just as they were handed down to us by those who from the first were eyewitnesses and servants of the word. Therefore, since I myself have carefully investigated everything from the beginning, it seemed good also to me to write an orderly account for you, most excellent Theophilus, so that you may know the certainty of the things you have been taught." (Luke 1:1-4)

It is important to realize that these writers had nothing to gain except criticism, persecution, prison, beatings, and death. It simply does not make sense that these men would be prepared to die for a message they knew to be false. Surely, if these writers were intentionally fabricating stories about Jesus, they would have confessed this deception once the brutal persecution of Christians began.

6) The presence of details which would embarrass the apostles support the Gospel's historicity.

When a writer is recording a story that includes his or her own actions and behavior, there is usually a temptation to make oneself look good. If the apostles were just "making it all up," why would they include that they disbelieved, misunderstood, and even denied Jesus? Why would they record that they childishly argued at times and often acted like selfish cowards?

7) The testimony of early non-Christian writers confirms the general information of Christ's life.

Lee Strobel in *The Case for Faith* reminds us of the following:

> "We have better historical documentation for Jesus than for the founder of any other ancient religion... One expert documented thirty-nine ancient sources (outside of the Bible) that corroborate more than one hundred facts concerning Jesus' life, teachings, crucifixion, and resurrection." [93]

Ancient writers and historians did not write much about religious matters. They usually wrote about political rulers, emperors, kings, military leaders, and battles. With this in mind, it is remarkable how much is recorded about Jesus and His followers by ancient non-Christian writers. For example, the Roman historian Cornelius Tacitus (A.D. *c.* 56–*c.* 120), who despised the Christian faith, affirmed that Jesus had suffered under Pontius Pilate. [94] Also, the governor of Bithynia (from A.D. 111 to 113) named Plinius Secundus (also known as Pliny the Younger) wrote the following description of Christians in a letter to Emperor Trajan:

> "...they were in the habit of meeting on a certain fixed day before it was light, when they sang an anthem to Christ as God, and bound themselves by a solemn oath not to commit any wicked deed, but to abstain from all fraud, theft and adultery, never to break their word, or deny a trust when called upon to honor it; after which it was their custom to separate, and then meet again to partake of food, but food of an ordinary kind." [95]

Thallus, another Roman historian who wrote close to the time of Jesus' life, made an interesting reference to the darkness over the land following Jesus' crucifixion. [96]

Flavius Josephus (A.D. *c.* 37–*c.* 100) was a Jewish historian who was born just a few years after Jesus died. In his famous writings, we find several references to people, places, and events that support the reliability of the New Testament, the most intriguing (and most controversial) being his account of the crucifixion of Jesus. In Josephus' writing entitled *Antiquities of the Jewish People* (A.D. 93), we find the following paragraph:

> And there arose about this time Jesus, a wise man, if indeed we should call him a man; for he was a doer of marvelous deeds, a teacher of men who received the truth with pleasure. He led away many Jews, and also many of the Greeks. This man was the Christ. And when Pilate had condemned him to the cross on his impeachment by the chief men among us, those who had loved him at first did not cease, the divine prophets having spoken these and thousands of other wonderful things about him; and even now the tribe of Christians, so named after him, has not yet died out.[97]

8) Archaeology has confirmed the circumstantial details in the New Testament.

As has already been mentioned, the distinguished Jewish archaeologist, Nelson Glueck has commented, "It may be stated categorically that no archaeological discovery has ever controverted a biblical reference. Scores of archaeological findings have been made which confirm in clear outline or exact detail historical statements in the Bible."[98] There have been many important recent archaeological finds that are relevant to the New Testament. Skeptics used to question the authenticity of the Gospels by pointing out that there was no external evidence that key New Testament figures, such as Pontius Pilate or the High Priest Caiaphas ever really existed. However, in 1962, while excavating at the ruins of Caesarea Maritima, archaeologists uncovered a first-century plaque with an inscription written in Latin bearing Pontius Pilate's name. Likewise, in 1990, an ossuary (a burial bone box) was discovered in a first-century burial chamber in Jerusalem with the words *Yehosef bar Qayafa* –'Joseph, son of Caiaphas'– etched on it. Experts believe that these words are most likely referring to Caiaphas, the Jewish High Priest who interrogated Jesus before His crucifixion.

9) The testimony of other early Christian writers supports most of the rest of the details about the life of Christ and His followers.

In addition to the vast amount of early New Testament manuscripts, we also have a multitude of writings and sermons written by early Christians containing quotations from the New Testament. In fact, there are so many of these quotations (around 86,000 in all!) that the New Testament could virtually be pieced together from them even if no other manuscript existed.

The skeptic may ask, "How can anyone possibly trust these writings when the authors were so blatantly biased toward Christianity?" In response, it is important to point out that these early Christian writers were people who had left their former lives and faith practices. In other words, they had not always been Christians. They all had non-Christian backgrounds and traditions and *then* became followers of Christ. Yes, they were biased, enthusiastic witnesses who wanted to persuade people, but this should not diminish the trustworthiness of their testimony. Rather, it is natural to wonder, *Why were these early Christian writers so enthusiastic about their message that they were willing to die for it?* The most plausible explanation is that these early writers had in some way experienced the power of God.

Before moving on to discuss the Old Testament, let us consider some final questions about the New Testament:

- If the New Testament stories are not authentic, factual accounts of the life of Jesus of Nazareth, then where do these stories come from?

- How do we explain the existence and the brilliance of the New Testament?

- Could uneducated fishermen simply make up the story of the Prodigal Son (found in Luke 15), which Charles Dickens once called the greatest piece of literature ever written?

- Could a group of liars compose the Sermon on the Mount (found in Matthew 5-7) which is universally praised as the pinnacle of ethical teaching?

The English reformer, Thomas Watson memorably addressed these types of questions when he wrote:

"I wonder whence the scripture should come if not from God. Bad men could not be the authors of it. Would their minds be employed in dictating such holy lines? Would they declare so freely against sin? Could good men be the authors of it? Could they write in such a strain? Or could it stand with their grace to counterfeit God's name and put 'thus saith the Lord' to a book of their own devising?"[99]

Now, let's consider the trustworthiness of the Old Testament.

When it comes to the Old Testament, it is the careful copying techniques of the ancient scribes that can give us confidence that the original message has been accurately and faithfully preserved.

"Hasn't the Bible changed over time?"

Imagine that the year is 1631. You decide to go down to the local market to purchase a Bible that has just been printed in English. After purchasing this Bible, you decide that the first thing you would like to do is to gather the family together for a reading of the Ten Commandments. *"Thou shalt not take the name of the Lord thy God in vain." "Thou shalt remember the Sabbath and keep it holy." "Honor your father and mother that your days may be prolonged."* You finally get down to the seventh commandment and read… *"Thou shalt commit adultery."* While one of your family members gasps for air, another fetches your reading glasses.

Embarrassed by your obvious mistake, you put the glasses on, clear your throat and read the seventh commandment once again: "Thou shalt commit adultery."

This is what an Old English, 1631 translation of the Bible would have said. For obvious reasons, that particular translation became known as the "wicked Bible" and the printer was punished by the King of England for this unfortunate printing oversight.

Many of us have enjoyed playing "the telephone game." You whisper a sentence or a short story into someone's ear and he, in turn, whispers the message into someone else's ear. On and on it goes until the last person has to report the message he or she has received. Most of the time, the final story is markedly different than the original.

What evidence do we have that the same sort of thing did not happen with the message of the Bible over the years? What confidence do we have that the originally intended content of the Bible has not been edited, corrupted, altered, or changed?

An important point to remember is that when the Bible is translated into English or any another language, scholars do not use more recent versions or translations as their source. Rather, they use the oldest and most reliable manuscripts of the Old and New Testament.

Also, consider what has been learned about the careful copying techniques used in transmitting the Bible.

Careful Copying Techniques:

The ancient scribes who copied the Bible were highly educated, trained professionals with strict standards, practices, and rules. For example, the rules for the Talmudists, who reproduced Old

Testament manuscripts from A.D. 270 to A.D. 500, included the following:

- The scribe must sit in full Jewish dress and be recently bathed.

- He should not begin to write the name of God with a pen newly dropped in ink.

- If a king addresses the scribe while writing the name of God, the scribe should ignore him.

- If there was one mistake on a scroll that was intended to be a master copy, it was destroyed.

- No word or letter could be written from memory without the scribe looking at the codex before him.

- Only a master copy could be used from which the scribe must not deviate—no duplicates of duplicates were allowed.

- Between every consonant the width of a hair or thread must intervene.

- Between every section, the breadth of nine consonants must intervene.

- Between every book, three lines must intervene.

- The fifth book of Moses must terminate exactly with a line, but the rest need not do so.[100]

The Massoretes (A.D. 500-900), who followed the Talmudists, likewise exercised great care in copying the Scriptures. Frederick Kenyon noted the following about the Massoretes in his work entitled *Our Bible and the Ancient Manuscripts*:

"They numbered the verses, words, and letters of every book. They calculated the middle verse, the middle word and the middle letter of each. They enumerated verses which contained all the letters of the alphabet, or a certain number of them; and so on. These trivialities, as we may rightly consider them, had yet the effect of securing minute attention to the precise transmission of the text; and they are but an excessive manifestation of a respect for the sacred scriptures which in itself deserves nothing but praise. The Massoretes were indeed anxious that not one jot nor tittle, not one smallest letter nor one tiny part of a letter, of the Law should pass away or be lost." [101]

Further regulations these ancient scribes adhered to were as follows: [102]

- They could only use clean animal skins to write on.
- Every skin must contain the same number of columns throughout the entire codex.
- They could have no less than forty eight and no more than sixty lines on a page.
- The ink must be black of a special recipe.
- They must verbalize aloud each word while they were writing it.
- They must wipe the pen and wash their entire bodies before writing the word "God."
- If three pages required correction, the entire document must be replaced.
- The letters, words, and paragraphs must be counted and compared to the standard.
- The document becomes invalid if two letters touch each other.
- All documents could only be stored in sacred places.
- All old and worn documents were buried with ceremonial pomp.

"Who decided which books to include in the Bible?"

As we have seen, the Bible claims that its authors were inspired by the Holy Spirit as they wrote the Word of God, and they were forbidden to add or subtract from it. [103] It is important to realize that a writing that had been inspired by God had authority from the moment it was written. As books that bore the obvious marks of inspiration were written, they were immediately treated with respect and regarded as authoritative. Copies were then made and shared with other groups of believers, and collections of these sacred writings began to accumulate and circulate.

Throughout the centuries, many have had questions not having to do with the accuracy of the Bible, but about which books belong and which books don't. This important issue was recently brought to the forefront because of the phenomenal success of Dan Brown's book, *The Da Vinci Code* which claims that the Roman Emperor Constantine "commissioned and financed a new Bible, which omitted those gospels that spoke of Christ's human traits and embellished those gospels that made him godlike."[104]

How do we respond to such assertions? How do we know that the Bible is complete? Who decided what books to include in the Bible? How do we know that only the sixty-six books in our Bible should be there? How do we know that some books aren't missing and that no more are being written? Why does the Catholic Bible have more books than the Protestant Bible? What should I say when someone claims to have a more recent written revelation from God?

These questions have to do with what we call the *canon.* The word *canon* comes from the Greek term used to describe a measuring rod or a "standard of measurement." The word eventually came to mean the official list of books that were recognized as being inspired by God and authoritative as God-given writings. There are great misconceptions about the canon. It is important to emphasize that the canonization of the books in the Bible was not a formal process that took place when a group of powerful church officials met to decide which writings to include and which to exclude. A book of the Bible is not "canon" because church councils arbitrarily decided which books would be authoritative. Instead, some early church councils officially *recognized* and *confirmed* the books which were already, obviously inspired and authoritative. In other words, the Bible does not owe its authority to any church, council or man. One writer put it this way, "a book is not the Word of God because it was accepted by the people of God. Rather, it was accepted by the people of God because it is the Word of God."

From the writings of the early church we can note at least five questions that guided the recognition and collection of the biblical books:

1) Was the book written by a prophet of God?

2) Was the writer confirmed by acts or miracles of God?

3) Did the message tell the truth about God?

4) Did the writing contain the power of God (such as fulfilled prophecy)?

5) Was the writing universally accepted by the people of God?

For example, Exodus 24:4 says, "Moses then wrote down everything the Lord had said." When Moses produced the Torah (also known as the Five Books of Moses or the Pentateuch), there was no need for anyone to pronounce his writings canonical, inspired or authoritative. Moses was already clearly recognized as the undisputed leader of the nation of Israel and several miraculous signs had unquestionably confirmed that God was speaking through him. Thus, his writings were immediately regarded as the very words of God.

What about the Apocrypha?

If you pick up a Roman Catholic Bible, you will find that it contains several additional Old Testament books. Catholicism and Protestantism are united in their acceptance of the twenty seven books of the New Testament, but concerning the Old Testament books there is a disagreement. These extra books are generally called the apocrypha. The Old Testament apocrypha includes books written during the period from around 200 B.C. to A.D. 200.[105] Interestingly, it was not until April 8, 1546 at the Council of Trent that these books were officially added to the Roman Catholic Bible.

Why are the apocryphal books rejected?

- None of them enjoyed universal recognition.
- They do not claim to be inspired and some specifically deny that they are inspired.
- They were not written by prophets.
- They were not confirmed by miracles.
- They contain no new supernatural prophecies.
- They were not accepted by early Jewish and Christian writers.
- They have been shrouded with continual uncertainty.
- These books were never accepted by the Jews as Scripture.
- They are not found in the Hebrew Bible.
- They contain false teachings, historical, and geographical mistakes.
- They teach doctrines that disagree with other books in the Bible.
- They don't "ring true." The quality of the literature is below that of the canonized literature.
- They lack the distinctive elements that give genuine Scripture its divine character, such as prophetic power.
- There is overwhelming historical testimony of their exclusion.
- Virtually, every Old Testament book is quoted from in the New Testament by Jesus or the apostles. Yet, Jesus never quoted the apocryphal writings in the New Testament.

What About The New Testament Canon?

The case for the New Testament canon is somewhat different. The New Testament was written over a short span of about fifty years (roughly from A.D. 45 to A.D. 95). The New Testament canon appears to have developed naturally and rapidly. The books of the New Testament were, for the most part, immediately recognized as inspired, and there was little controversy about them.

Amy Orr-Ewing of the Oxford Centre for Christian Apologetics helps us here:

> "The wide circulation of the New Testament and the sheer numbers of churches involved in reading and propagating it acted as a protection against forgery and fraud, as any interloper would have had to convince large numbers of people across a vast geographical area... The manuscript tradition of the New Testament is preserved in great numbers from different places around the globe. We have distinct streams of manuscripts which come to us now from the time of the events they record and preserved in different languages—the same text of the New Testament with minor differences in spelling and occasionally different words."[106]

We do find in early church documents that the New Testament books were recognized as authoritative based on the following criteria:

1) The document should be written by an apostle or a close associate of an apostle.

2) The writer should be approved by the recognized apostles.

3) The document should be universally recognized as authoritative.

It is comforting to know that the early church and early Christian writers listed the exact twenty-seven books we now recognize as the New Testament. The earliest example of a complete list of the New Testament books can be found in a letter to the churches by Athanasius of Alexandria written in A.D. 367. There were, in fact, church councils (called synods) that convened for the purpose of counteracting early heresies (such as the Synod of Hippo in A.D. 393 and in Carthage in A.D. 397) and at these meetings church leaders officially recognized the twenty-seven New Testament books. However, it should again be emphasized that these church leaders did not *choose* these books, but rather they *recognized* and publicly *confirmed* the obvious authority, beauty, and inspiration these sacred writings already possessed.

How do we know that the New Testament is complete and the canon is closed?

We can be sure that the biblical canon is closed because Jesus limited the teaching authority to His apostles, who all died before the end of the first century. Just before Jesus was killed, He promised to guide His apostles into all truth saying, "But the Counselor, the Holy Spirit, whom the Father will send in my name, will teach you all things and will remind you of everything I have said to you" (John 14:26). Again, in John 16:13, Jesus comforts His disciples by saying, "But when he, the Spirit of truth, comes, he will guide you into all truth." This is the reason that, from the very beginning, the church "devoted themselves to the apostles teaching" (Acts 2:42) and why the church is said to be "built on the foundation of the apostles and prophets" (Ephesians 2:20). The twenty-seven books of the New Testament are the only authentic record of the apostle's teaching in existence.

"What about all the contradictions in the Bible?"

Dr. Gleason Archer, (a Harvard graduate who has taught graduate-level seminary in the field of Biblical criticism and has learned over 30 languages, most of them languages of Old Testament times in the Middle Eastern world) in his book entitled *Encyclopedia of Bible Difficulties* said this:

"As I have dealt with one apparent discrepancy after another and have studied the alleged contradictions between the biblical record and the evidence of linguistics, archaeology, or science, my confidence in the trustworthiness of Scripture has been repeatedly verified and strengthened by the discovery that almost every problem in Scripture that has ever been discovered by man, from ancient times until now, has been dealt with in a completely satisfactory manner by the biblical text itself—or else by objective archaeological information." [107]

Dr. Norman Geisler has made it a hobby of collecting "alleged conflicts or mistakes" in the Bible. In fact, he has written a book called *"When Critics Ask"* in which he devoted more than 570 pages to the "alleged contradictions or mistakes." Dr. Geisler said this:

"I have a list of about 800 of them. Of the 800 allegations I've studied, I haven't found one single error in the Bible, but I've found a lot of errors by the critics… When it has been proven to be accurate over and over again in hundreds of details, the burden of proof is on the critic, not the Bible." [108]

CHAPTER 8

Why Is There Suffering and Evil?

In her book entitled *When God Weeps*, Joni Eareckson Tada writes the following about her friend, John McAllister, whose degenerative nerve disease leaves him bedridden and unable to move:

> "Nighttime is no longer friendly. Shadows cast jerking, jagging shapes across the room. Gravity is his enemy as the weight of the air settles on his chest. Breathing is heavy labor. Calling out is impossible. He needs to call out tonight. In the darkness an ant finds him. The scout sends for others and they come. First hundreds, then thousands. A noiseless legion inches its way down the chimney, across the floor, secretly crawling up his urine tube, up, over and onto his bed. They fan out over the hills and valleys of John's blanket, tunneling under and onto his body. He is covered by a black, wriggling, invasion... John's wife, along with a nurse, found him in the early morning with ants still in his hair, mouth, and eyes. His skin was badly bitten and burned... John is a Christian. His God can see in the dark. Why, in the name of heaven, why? God, who are you?... This is suffering stalking a person down and ripping into his sanity. This is affliction spinning out of control... Is this God's idea of accomplishing something deep and profound in our lives? Is there anyone out there who can make sense of this? Who actually believes this?"[109]

Millions upon millions of similar, horrific stories like this, as well as personal experiences with suffering, have driven scores of people to question God's character, justice, power, goodness, and love. Peter De Vries describes the age-old mystery of pain as "the question mark turned like a fishhook in the human heart." [110] The jagged edges of the reality of suffering and evil in the world have even led many to deduce that an all-powerful, all-loving God cannot possibly exist.

The Christian lecturer, Michael Ramsden succinctly sums up the problem of suffering this way: "For a while now, at least in the Western world, the existence of any form of pain, suffering or evil has been regarded as evidence for the non-existence of God. If a good God existed, people say, these things wouldn't. But they do and, therefore, he doesn't." Nineteenth-century minister, Joseph Parker, conveyed these feelings with forthright honesty, anguish, and anger following the death of his wife:

> "In that dark hour, I became almost an atheist. For God had set his foot upon my prayers and treated my petitions with contempt. If I had seen a dog in such agony as mine, I would have pitied and helped the dumb beast; yet God spat upon me and cast me out as an offence—out into the waste wilderness and the night black and starless." [111]

Stating The Problem [112]

The presence of suffering and evil in the world undoubtedly presents the single greatest challenge to the Christian faith. Henri Blocher, commenting on this challenge, writes, "while it is evil that tortures human bodies, it is the problem of evil that torments the human mind." [113] Even the prophets in the Bible raise the question in various forms. For example, the prophet Habakkuk asked God, "How long, O Lord, must I call for help, but you do not listen? Or cry out to you, 'Violence!' but you do not save? Why do you make me look at injustice? Why do you tolerate wrong?" (Habakkuk 1:2-3) Jeremiah challenged God by saying, "I would speak with you about your justice: why does the way of the wicked prosper?" (Jeremiah 12:1) However the issue is articulated, it is ultimately God's character and moral trustworthiness that are called into question.

Some Important Points To Begin With

It is important to say at the outset that when examining the question of suffering and evil we should have a proper degree of humility and realize that we are dealing with a profound mystery for which no one has an exhaustively satisfying answer. The human mind seeking to explain this mystery is like a harmonica interpreting Beethoven. The music is too majestic for the instrument. Further, it must be acknowledged that every world religion and worldview must give an explanation for evil and suffering. This is not just a Christian question. Finally, it should be pointed out that if someone puts forth an explanation for the problem of suffering and evil, it should make sense logically, intellectually, philosophically, and emotionally.

What Are The Possible Answers?

Let us begin by examining and evaluating how other worldviews go about formulating a response to the mystery of suffering and evil.

One way that people choose to resolve this problem is to say that evil and suffering really do not exist. Many Eastern religions go this route. For example, many pantheistic[114] religions teach, *"If God is all, and God is good, then evil can not exist."* Hinduism, Taoism, some forms of Buddhism, the Christian Science Church, Unitarians, and others teach that the way to resolve the problem of evil is to realize that it really does not exist at all. It is an illusion. Thus, in order to overcome pain, suffering, and evil, we must learn to believe that everything in the physical world is non-real—then the illusion will have no grip on us.

Many would contend that this explanation does not make sense emotionally. I can't imagine having to tell a rape victim, "The evil and pain you have encountered is just an illusion."

It could also be argued that the pantheistic explanation of evil and suffering does not make sense intellectually. Ravi Zacharias tells the humorous story of India's leading philosopher, Shankara who had just finished lecturing the king on the deception of the mind and its delusion of material reality when an elephant went on a rampage. Promptly, Shankara climbed up a tree to find safety. When the king asked him why he ran if the elephant was non-real, Shankara, not to be outdone, said, "What the king actually saw was a non-real me climbing up a non-real tree!" Zacharias offers this addendum: "One might add, 'this is a non-real answer.'"[115]

Another example of an explanation that does not make sense logically or emotionally is atheism. Atheism puts forth the following response to the question of human suffering: "We are living in an impersonal, accidental universe in which some people get lucky and others don't. There is no point of thinking of a creator-god to whom we can attribute goodness or badness —it is all matter plus time plus chance. We are all simply part of a cosmic casino and no questions should be asked."[116]

Many atheists and skeptics begin their challenge to God's existence by saying, *"God can't exist because evil exists."* However, there are logical problems with this statement. Consider the following dialogue by Ravi Zacharias and a university student from a question and answer session:[117]

Student: There is too much evil in this world; therefore, there cannot be a God!

Speaker: Would you mind if I asked you something? You said, "God cannot exist because there is too much evil." If there is such a thing as evil, aren't you assuming that there is such a thing as good?

Student: I guess so.

Speaker: When you accept the existence of goodness, you must affirm a moral law on the basis of which to differentiate between good and evil. But when you admit to a moral law, you must posit a moral lawgiver. That, however, is who you are trying to disprove and not prove. For, if there is no moral lawgiver, there is no moral law. If there is no moral law, there is no good. If there is no good, there is no evil. What, then, is your question?

Student: What, then, am I asking you?

This student just realized that the question of evil and suffering is only valid if God, in fact, exists. In other words, as soon as you take God out of the picture, terms like *good* and *evil* can only be defined by conflicting human opinions and personal feelings. If morality is defined by human opinion, we are reduced to asking ourselves, *Which human's opinion do we choose to follow?* "Seen in this light," Zacharias concludes, "the reality of evil actually requires the existence of God rather than disproves it."[118]

So, atheism's explanation for the problem of evil and suffering does not make sense logically. Also, it does not make sense emotionally. Listen to what Oxford University professor, Richard Dawkins, says about why people suffer:

> "In a universe of blind physical forces and genetic replication, some people are going to get hurt, other people are going to get lucky, and you won't find any rhyme or reason in it, nor any justice. The universe we observe has precisely the properties we should expect if there is, at the bottom, no design, no purpose, no evil and no other good. Nothing but blind, pitiless indifference. DNA neither knows nor cares. DNA just is. And we dance to its music."[119]

Would Dawkins honestly tell a rape victim that the rapist was merely dancing to his DNA?[120]

We have seen that non-Christian worldviews struggle to give us satisfactory answers to the problem of suffering and evil. Let us now consider the Christian position on this mystery. If it is true that the question of evil is valid only if God exists, how can the stark reality of suffering in the world possibly be reconciled with the Christian affirmation that God is sovereign, just, and good?

"Why did God create a world where evil and suffering exists?"

Most human suffering can be put into two broad categories:

1) Suffering caused by moral evil or sin.

2) Suffering brought on by natural causes.

When examining the question of responsibility and origin of these two categories, it is helpful to consider the possible worlds God could have created.

Think about four possible worlds God could have created:

1. God could have created no world at all

Would a non-world be better than our world? Though this might be an interesting question for philosophers to wrestle with, it is not helpful to our discussion, for "something" and "nothing" cannot be compared. As Norman Geisler put it, it is like "comparing apples and non-apples, insisting that non-apples taste better."[121]

2. God could have created a world where only goodness could be chosen

In this type of world, suffering caused by moral evil or human sin would not exist. Although this sounds wonderful at first glance, the result of creating this type of world would be the negation of free choice. In fact, if God created a non-moral world, it would also be a non-free world. Freedom of choice is necessary if the word *morality* is to have any meaning. Again, Geisler sums this up well: "A non-moral world cannot be morally better than a moral world."

If God did not create us with the freedom to choose, we would be like robots. Certainly, God could have created humans who had no choice to love him or not. This, however, would have made real love impossible. For example, imagine a man who programmed his computer to say *"I love you!"* every few minutes. Would this be real love?

One of the greatest gifts God has given us is the freedom and ability to choose. However, free choice always leaves the possibility of a wrong choice. "Not even an all-powerful God," John Stott reminds us, "could give man freedom and at the same time guarantee that he would use it wisely."[122] In other words, "it is not possible to force people to freely choose the good. Forced freedom is a contradiction."[123] In his celebrated book, *Mere Christianity,* C.S. Lewis writes,

> "God created things which had free will. That means creatures which can go either wrong or right. Some people think they can imagine a creature which was free but had no possibility of going wrong; I cannot. If a thing is free to be good it is also free to be bad. And free will is what has made evil possible. Why then, did God give them free will? Because free will, though it makes evil possible, is the only thing that makes possible any love or goodness or joy worth having. A world of automata—of creatures that worked like machines—would hardly be worth creating."[124]

God does not force us to love Him or obey Him. If we choose to love God, it should follow that we will seek to obey Him. If everyone chose to love and obey God, evil would not result. If people choose not to obey God, evil will result. This is where suffering caused by evil comes from. It comes from disobedience and the misuse of freedom. It does not come from God.

The Nature of Evil

As we consider the issue of free will, another question emerges that needs to be addressed: If God created everything and evil is a "thing" with which humans are confronted, can't we deduce that God created evil?

In addressing this question it is good to carefully consider the nature of evil. Christian thinkers, such as Augustine and Thomas Aquinas helped develop the idea that evil should not be defined as a "thing" or an "initial ingredient of existence"[125] but, rather, the absence of something. Michael Ramsden offers this helpful illustration: In order to make a room dark, we do not switch the darkness on—we switch the light off. Darkness is a negative entity that can be explained only as the absence of light. So it is with evil. Negative entities are not created.

This understanding of the nature of evil is in harmony with the first chapters of the Bible, which teach that in the beginning God created a good world without suffering and uncontaminated by evil. Genesis 1:31 tells us, "God saw all that he had made, and it was very good." Angelic beings were also created as a part of God's good creation. Finally, God created human beings and blessed them with the capacity to love, grow, learn, and mature. To do this, it was necessary to create an environment where individuals possessed the freedom to obey or disobey, love or ignore their Creator. A particular created spirit called Satan—who was not created as evil—at some point, misused the freedom he was given and chose to rebel against God's authority.[126] This "fallen angel" eventually tempted Adam and Eve to disobey God, and "sin entered the world" (Romans 5:12). Evil and suffering were now a part of human existence. Thus, according to the Bible, suffering caused by evil is an "alien intrusion into God's good world"[127] and "arises from the misuse of created freedom, that of the devil and then that of human beings."[128]

3. God could have created a world without suffering due to natural causes

A third possible world God could have created is one in which there was no such thing as suffering due to natural causes. As we have seen, the original creation is described in Genesis as being "very good." This implies that events such as tsunamis, hurricanes, cancer, or death due to natural causes would not have been a concern. However, when Adam and Eve misused their freedom, the results were catastrophic. Humanity became alienated internally (with shame, guilt, fear, anxiety), spiritually (with God), socially (with others), vocationally (with work) and even ecologically (with nature). Death, disease, and decay not only became a part of the human experience, but nature itself became contaminated. We now live in a fallen world where even the ground is cursed (Genesis 3:17-19). Because of sin, we are subject to suffering because of natural causes that would not have occurred had humans remained obedient to God. John Blanchard writes, "the world as we now see it is not in its original condition, but it is radically ruined by sin, and we live on what someone has called a 'stained planet.'"[129] The Bible describes it this way:

"For the creation was subjected to frustration, not by its own choice, but by the will of the one who subjected it, in hope that the creation itself will be liberated from its bondage to decay and brought into the freedom and glory of the children of God. We know that the whole creation has been groaning as in the pains of childbirth right up to the present time." (Romans 8:18-22)

4. Our World

The forth possible world to consider is the world as we know it—where good and evil exist along with the possibility of choosing either. In his classic commentary on the problem of pain, C. S. Lewis writes the following:

"We want…not so much a Father in Heaven as a grandfather in heaven—a senile benevolence who, as they say, 'liked to see young people enjoying themselves' and whose plan for the universe was simply that it might be truly said at the end of each day, 'a good time was had by all'… I should very much like to live in a universe which was governed on such lines. But since it is abundantly clear that I don't, and since I have reason to believe, nevertheless, that God is Love, I conclude that my conception of love needs correction."[130]

This marvelous quotation brings up an important question—What was God's purpose for creating everything in the first place? If God's intention was to produce an environment where free humans could develop character and grow in their love for God and each other, then He succeeded. In the final analysis, of the four worlds described—ours is the only one where love is possible.[131] Norman Geisler summarizes this point well:

> "This world is the **best way** to the **best world.** If God is to both preserve freedom and defeat evil, then this world is the best way to do it. Freedom is preserved in that each person makes his or her own free choice to determine their destiny. Evil is overcome in that once those who reject God are separated from the others, the decisions of all are honored and made permanent."[132]

The Question of Permission

Thus far, I have hoped to show that when looking for someone to blame for the origin of evil and suffering, we are not in a position to point an accusing finger at God. There is, however, another troubling question that emerges: Why does God *permit* so much suffering and evil in our world? Can't partial blame be attributed to someone who has the ability to stop suffering, yet does not do so?

To address this question, let us now turn to the classic biblical case study on the problem of suffering—the book of Job. Although Job's saga supplies no exhaustive or definitive answer to the problem of evil and pain, there are many crucial teachings that are relevant to our discussion. Job is introduced as a good, blameless, upright, wealthy man who "feared God and shunned evil." Meanwhile, in a heavenly dialogue with God, Satan insinuates that the reason Job is so good and faithful is because he has been blessed with a great family, great riches, and great health. In response, God permits Satan to test Job and violent waves of death, destruction and carnage begin to crash in on Job's life. In a matter of hours, Job loses his livestock, servants, and children. Yet, "in all this, Job did not sin by charging God with wrongdoing" (Job 1:22). So, Satan again challenged God, "…stretch out your hand and strike his flesh and bones, and he will surely curse you to your face" (Job 2:4). Again, God allowed Satan to test Job. "So Satan went out from the presence of the Lord and afflicted Job with painful sores from the soles of his feet to the top of his head" (Job 2:7).

What can we learn from this episode about affixing blame for human suffering? Who is responsible for Job's suffering?

The book of Job investigates this question in depth. Job, himself, is interrogated throughout as a possible suspect. "Surely, these things wouldn't be happening if Job was not hiding some secret sin," reasoned Job's "comforters." However, the message of the book teaches just the opposite. If "Job's sinfulness" is not to blame, what is? We could certainly identify wicked people—the Sabeans (Job 1:15) and the Chaldeans (Job 1:17)—and bad weather—presumably lightening (Job 1:16) and a great wind (Job 1:19)—as the culprits. On a deeper level, Satan is clearly to blame.[133] Yet, it is the deepest level of understanding that is so troubling. Yes, the direct blame should go to bad people, bad weather, and a bad angel. However, this does not tell the whole story. Indirectly, does not God share part of the blame? It is the awareness that God Himself allowed, and even authorized, Job's sufferings that is so unsettling. What are we to make of this?

First of all, this is not an issue that is particular to the book of Job. God's supreme authority over all that happens on earth is a consistent teaching throughout Scripture. Indeed, whatever we can think of in this world that brings about suffering, we can find a biblical verse claiming God's sovereignty over it.

Second, if we are disturbed by the idea that God screens evil, consider how disconcerting it would be to find out that He *didn't*. Steven Estes responds to God's sovereignty in light of Job's suffering this way:

"Satan acted freely; no one forced his hand. God's reaction to the devil was merely to lengthen his leash... What's clear immediately is that God permits all sorts of things he doesn't approve of... Do we find repulsive a God who gives the nod to our tragedies? What if your trials weren't screened by any divine plan? Try to conceive of Lucifer unrestrained. Left to his own, the Devil would make Jobs of us all... If God didn't control evil, the result would be evil uncontrolled. God permits what he hates to achieve what he loves."[134]

Could it be that God allowed the tragic events we read about in the book of Job to show humanity what it would be like if He let go of Satan's leash? Is it possible that these events were recorded in Scripture so that everyone could vividly witness what the devil is really like and the suffering that he would inflict without God's restraining? Perhaps, the book of Job is an inspired glimpse of what hell is like and, just briefly, God deemed it necessary to pull back the curtain so that we could get a good look at the true character of this fallen angel with whom we so flippantly flirt.

Job never received an exhaustive, theoretical answer as to why he was suffering. It is unlikely that a "reason" would have satisfied him anyway. In the end, the only thing that could fill the void in Job's afflicted life was the presence of God. Indeed, the very thing that Job wanted and needed most was given to him—the opportunity to see God. Rather than revealing any ultimate "solution" to the problem of pain, God reveals himself. For Job, this was enough, as is evident in his response, "My ears had heard of you but now my eyes have seen you. Therefore I despise myself and repent in dust and ashes" (Job 42:5-6).

The book of Job illustrates that "it is less important to know all the answers than to know and trust the one who does."[135] Job's saga ends with God presenting him sixty-two questions. These questions seem to have answered Job's. But, do they answer ours? Rather than thundering out unanswerable questions at a wounded man, wouldn't it be more meaningful if God came down from the safety and comfort of heaven—into our world—and had to experience our pain? What if God actually accepted the blame and the punishment for the evil in our world? It is here that the Christian gospel becomes extremely relevant to our discussion.

CHAPTER 9

What Is
God's Response to Evil?

In this chapter, we will consider the problem of suffering and evil from a biblical perspective and offer several points brought out by Scripture, culminating with the Christian affirmation that God, Himself, entered our world, experienced our pain, accepted the blame for our evil, and took our punishment.

Biblical Perspectives On Suffering And Evil

1. Suffering can develop our character and lead us to maturity.

Suffering is not always evil. Often, it is a good thing in the human experience and essential for our survival. The pain sensors in our central nervous system serve as necessary warning signals. Without them our lives would be "fraught with danger, and devoid of many basic pleasures."[136] Dr. Paul Brand, one of the world's leading experts on leprosy, discovered that the most dangerous aspect of this disease is actually the absence of pain. The more pain that is muffled in a person's body, Brand's research revealed, the more likely that person will destroy it. Pain not only serves to protect the body, but also to strengthen it. For example, have you ever watched a butterfly struggling to get free from a cocoon? It certainly doesn't look like it is having a good time. In fact, it looks like it is suffering. However, if we feel sorry for it, intervene, and tear the cocoon open to set the butterfly free, it will die. The struggle strengthens the butterfly so it can survive. The same type of thing could be said about a human's physical, mental, emotional, and spiritual development as the following New Testament verse points out:

> "Consider it pure joy, my brothers, whenever you face trials of many kinds, because you know that the testing of your faith develops perseverance. Perseverance must finish its work so that you may be mature and complete, not lacking anything." (James 1:2-4)

Someone once asked the great Renaissance sculptor Michelangelo, "How can you take a huge hunk of granite and turn it into David?" He reportedly answered, "That hunk of granite *is* David. I just have to remove everything that does not belong." How can God take a sinful, imperfect, flawed human being and make him into a mature, complete, holy, blameless, Christ-like person? God has to remove everything that does not belong, and that process, though necessary, is often painful. At times, God uses affliction "like a hammer and chisel, chipping and cutting to reveal his image in you. God chooses as his model his Son, Jesus Christ." [137]

2. Suffering helps us realize that we need God.

> "God whispers to us in our pleasures, speaks in our conscience, but shouts in our pains. It is his megaphone to rouse a deaf world." [138]

This famous quote from C. S. Lewis reminds us that sometimes suffering is the only thing that has the potency to jolt us out of our attitude of self-sufficiency and turn us away from a path of destruction. The apostle Paul, no stranger to suffering, often acknowledged this in his writings, as we see in the following verse:

> "We do not want you to be uninformed, brothers, about the hardships we suffered in the province of Asia. We were under great pressure, far beyond our ability to endure, so that we despaired even of life. Indeed, in our hearts we felt the sentence of death. *But this happened that we might not rely on ourselves but on God, who raises the dead.*" (2 Corinthians 1:8-9)

Suffering can purify our faith, encourage holiness, promote humility, cause us to repent, and bring us closer to God. Paul recognized that the "thorn in his flesh" was to keep him "from becoming conceited" (2 Corinthians 12:7). Peter even goes on to say, "...he who has suffered in his body is done with sin" (1 Peter 4:1). The writer of Psalm 119 would agree, for he admitted, "before I was afflicted I went astray, but now I obey your word" (Psalm 119:67).

3. Our suffering can help us understand the suffering of others.

Paul writes, "Praise be to the God and Father of our Lord Jesus Christ, the Father of compassion and the God of all comfort, who comforts us in all our troubles, so that we can comfort those in any trouble with the comfort we ourselves have received from God. For just as the sufferings of Christ flow over into our lives, so also through Christ our comfort overflows" (2 Corinthians 1:3-5). For a wonderful example of this, see Donald W. Sublett's book titled *Head-And-Neck Cancer Kills... "Fight's On!"* http:/tinyurl.com/hewuwf7.

4. Sometimes we suffer because of personal sin.

> "Do not be deceived: God cannot be mocked. A man reaps what he sows. The one who sows to please his sinful nature, from that nature will reap destruction...." (Galatians 6:7-8)

We must not overlook the fact that many of our wounds are self-inflicted. A majority of the suffering in our world is directly caused by humans doing things that God commanded us not to do. The Bible is also clear that some suffering is due to God's discipline.[139] However, it is important to point out that Jesus rejected the idea that there is always a necessary direct correlation between our personal sin and our suffering.[140]

5. God never intended this world to be our ultimate home.

Suffering, says Joni Eareckson Tada, reminds us that we should never get too comfortable in this fallen world, which is destined for destruction and decay. She writes,

> "Earth's pain keeps crushing our hopes, reminding us that this world can never satisfy; only heaven can... Suffering keeps swelling our feet so that earth's shoes won't fit." [141]

In Hebrews 11, after recording a litany of faithful sufferers, the writer says this:

> "All these people were still living by faith when they died. They did not receive the things promised; they only saw them and welcomed them from a distance. And they admitted that they were aliens and strangers on earth... Instead, they were longing for a better country—a heavenly one. Therefore God is not ashamed to be called their God, for he has prepared a city for them." (Hebrews 11:13-16)

Paul adds these words of hope: "I consider that our present sufferings are not worth comparing with the glory that will be revealed in us" (Romans 8:18). "No eye has seen, no ear has heard, no mind has conceived what God has prepared for those who love him" (1 Corinthians 2:9).

6. Life and good health are gifts from God.

Why is it that we are so quick to question God's character when we are faced with hardship, yet scarcely acknowledge Him when enjoying good health and things are going well? Where does life and good health come from in the first place? The Bible clearly claims "all have sinned and fall short of the glory of God" and "the wages of sin is death" (Romans 3:23, 6:23). Therefore, if God were to eliminate all humanity this instant, He would not have compromised His justice or righteousness. The astonishing reality is that we are only alive today because God "does not treat us as our sins deserve or repay us according to our iniquities" (Psalm 103:10). [142]

7. Where is atheism when people suffer?

Christianity offers hope, peace, and comfort in the midst of affliction. What does atheism offer that comforts or gives hope when experiencing pain? The question is often raised, "Where was God during the Holocaust?" An appropriate response can be, "Where was atheism during the Holocaust? Was it not the natural outworking of atheism that fueled the Holocaust?"[143]

It would be appropriate here to discuss the Holocaust in further detail as it is extremely significant when discussing the problem of suffering and evil. Questions about the Holocaust are obviously difficult for anyone to address. What person from any religious background or worldview could confidently proclaim, "I have adequate and satisfactory answers to all the questions raised by the Holocaust?" The Holocaust has caused many to abandon the notion of an all-loving, all-powerful God. The Jewish author, Richard Rubenstein concluded, "...we stand in a cold, silent, unfeeling cosmos, unaided by any power beyond our own resources. After Auschwitz, what else can a Jew say about God?"[144]

What can Christians offer as a response to this? First of all, it is important to remember that Hitler's goals were clearly stated: "I freed Germany from the stupid and degrading fallacies of conscience and morality... We will train people before whom the world will tremble. I want young people capable of violence —imperious, relentless and cruel."[145] The Holocaust was planned and executed by people who were following a message that was the absolute antithesis of the Christian message.

The underlying issue raised by an event such as the Holocaust can be stated this way: The evil and wickedness during the Holocaust was at such an appalling level that God should have intervened.

How might we respond to such a statement? Perhaps we should consider the questions that would immediately emerge if God would have intervened and thwarted all attempts of evil during this time in history. If this "level of wickedness" was extracted from human history, what about the next level? What about the horrendous atrocities Joseph Stalin inflicted on his own people? Again, God could have foiled all plans of human wickedness during Stalin's regime—but, what about the next level of evil intentions, and the next, and the next? If God intervened and stripped away every "level" of evil and wickedness, it would soon get personal. Eventually, God would reach the level of evil in our hearts, minds, and behavior.

Years ago, *The Times* solicited a group of famous British writers to respond to the question, "What is wrong with the world?" The shortest and most profound reply was written by G.K. Chesterton. He wrote the following:

> "In response to your question, 'What's wrong with the world?' –
> I am. Yours faithfully,
>
> ~ G.K. Chesterton."[146]

Commenting on this issue, Michael Green offers the following insights:

> "Suppose for a moment that God were immediately to wipe out all evil? Would not humanity be destroyed? For which of us is free from evil? Far from remaining an abstract intellectual problem, evil is a very pressing moral problem within each of us. We ourselves are the problem of evil! And if simple eradication were the answer, we would have no hope."[147]

8. But... *"What about the death of a child?"*

"If God is good and can do anything, how do you explain the death of a child?"

First of all, it is important to be reminded that...

If there is *no God,* then there is *no explanation.*

If there is *no God,* there is *no answer* to this question.

If there is *no God,* when a child dies there is *no hope* for the family to ever see that child again.

However, from a Christian point of view, when a child dies the family can still have hope, peace, strength, and comfort. Here are four reasons why:

A. God created the child's life; He has the power to give the child life again.

The Bible tells about a man named Lazarus who died. His sister, Martha, went to talk to Jesus and said. "'Lord, if you had been here, my brother would not have died. But I know that even now God will give you whatever you ask.' Jesus said to her, 'Your brother will rise again.' Martha answered, 'I know he will rise again in the resurrection at the last day.' Jesus said to her, '**I am the resurrection and the life.** He who believes in me will live, even though he dies; and whoever lives and believes in me will never die. Do you believe this?'" (John 11:21-26)

B. When a child dies he or she goes to Heaven which is a better place than our world.

The apostle Paul stated, "For to me, to live is Christ and to die is gain. If I am to go on living in the body, this will mean fruitful labor for me. Yet what shall I choose? I do not know! I am torn between the two: **I desire to depart and be with Christ, which is better by far**" (Philippians 1:21-24).

The following verses indicate that when a child dies, he or she goes to be with God in Heaven: 2 Samuel 12:21-23; Matthew 18:2-4, 19:13-15; Romans 9:11; 1 Corinthians 14:20; Deuteronomy 1:39.

C. God can comfort the family who lost the child.

To the family and loved ones, God can be the comforter and healer. King David, who himself lost a child, wrote, "Even though I walk through the valley of the shadow of death, I will fear no evil, for you are with me; your rod and your staff they comfort me" (Psalm 23).

D. The Bible promises us that the separation caused by death is only temporary for those who are Christians.

"Brothers, we do not want you to be ignorant about those who fall asleep, or to grieve like the rest of men, who have no hope. We believe that Jesus died and rose again and so we believe that God will bring with Jesus those who have fallen asleep in him. According to the Lord's own word, we tell you that we who are still alive, who are left till the coming of the Lord, will certainly not precede those who have fallen asleep. For the Lord himself will come down from heaven, with a loud command, with the voice of the archangel and with the trumpet call of God, and the dead in Christ will rise first. After that, we who are still alive and are left will be caught up together with them in the clouds to meet the Lord in the air. And so we will be with the Lord forever. Therefore encourage each other with these words." (1 Thessalonians 4:13-18)

Helen Keller beautifully expressed the unquenchable hope of the Christian faith this way:

"For three things I thank God every day of my life: thanks that He has vouchsafed me knowledge of His works; deep thanks that He has set in my darkness the lamp of faith; deep, deepest thanks that I have another life to look forward to—a life joyous with light and flowers and heavenly song."

9. In Christ, all suffering is temporary.

The Bible encourages us with the following verses about heaven:

"Never again will they hunger; never again will they thirst. The sun will not beat upon them, nor any scorching heat. For the Lamb at the center of the throne will be their shepherd; he will lead them to springs of living water. And God will wipe away every tear from their eyes." (Revelation 7:13-17)

"And I heard a loud voice from the throne saying, 'Now the dwelling of God is with men, and he will live with them. They will be his people, and God himself will be with them and be their God. He will wipe every tear from their eyes. There will be no more death or mourning or crying or pain, for the old order of things has passed away.' He who was seated on the throne said, 'I am making everything new!'" (Revelation 21:3-5)

The Bible not only promises that everything in heaven will be new, pure, and unblemished, but also that God's resurrected children will be given new resurrected bodies. For example, the apostle Paul compares our earthly body as a seed. In 1 Corinthians 15:35-44, he writes,

"But someone may ask, 'How are the dead raised? With what kind of body will they come?' How foolish! What you sow does not come to life unless it dies. When you sow, you do not plant the body that will be, but just as a seed... So will it be with the resurrection of the dead. The body that is sown is perishable, it is raised imperishable; it is sown in dishonor, it is raised in glory; it is sown in weakness, it is raised in power; it is sown a natural body, it is raised a spiritual body."

In Philippians 3:21, Christians are promised that Christ will "transform our lowly bodies so that they will be like his glorious body." Commenting on these encouraging verses, Joni Eareckson Tada (who was disabled in a diving accident and is now a quadriplegic) writes,

"I still can hardly believe it. I, with shriveled, bent fingers, atrophied muscles, gnarled knees, and no feeling from the shoulders down, will one day have a new body, light, bright, and clothed in righteousness—powerful and dazzling. Can you imagine the hope this gives someone spinal-chord injured like me? Or someone who is cerebral palsied, brain-injured, or has multiple sclerosis? Imagine the hope this gives someone who is manic-depressive. No other religion, no other philosophy promises new bodies, hearts and minds. Only in the Gospel of Christ do hurting people find such incredible hope."[148]

10. God is not finished yet!

One of the unique features of the Christian faith is the assurance that although evil and suffering persists in our world today, they will be abolished in the future. Put another way, "the existence of evil does not eliminate the possibility of God, but the existence of God guarantees the elimination of evil."[149] Christians embrace the biblical teaching that justice delayed is not justice denied.[150] Peter Kreeft reminds us, "criticizing God for not punishing evil people right now is like reading half a novel and criticizing the author for not resolving the plot."[151]

> **"And we know that in all things**
> **God works for the good of those who love him,**
> **who have been called according to his purpose."**
> **(Romans 8:28)**

11. God experienced human suffering.

The book of Hebrews encourages those who suffer with these words, "For we do not have a high priest who is unable to sympathize with our weaknesses, but we have one who has been tempted in every way, just as we are—yet was without sin" (Hebrews 4:15). The Christian faith proclaims that God took the pain of His creation onto Himself. He entered our world of evil, temptation, and suffering in the person of Jesus Christ. Scripture tells us that Christ, "who, being in very nature God, did not consider equality with God something to be grasped, but made himself nothing, taking the very nature of a servant, being made in human likeness. And being found in appearance as a man, he humbled himself and became obedient to death—even death on a cross!" (Philippians 2:6-8) "He was despised and rejected by men, a man of sorrows, and familiar with suffering. Like one from whom men hide their faces he was despised, and we esteemed him not. Surely he took up our infirmities and carried our sorrows, yet we considered him stricken by God, smitten by him, and afflicted. But he was pierced for our transgressions, he was crushed for our iniquities; the punishment that brought us peace was upon him, and by his wounds we are healed" (Isaiah 53:2-5). These profound statements proclaim that God loves us so much that He chose to take on our condition and experience our suffering. While Jesus lived with us on earth, He became hungry, thirsty and tired (John 4:6, 19:28; Mark 4:38). He wept over the death of a friend (John 11:35). He knew temptation of every kind. He knew the agony of being lied about, betrayed, misunderstood, abandoned, abused, violated, and beaten. He even experienced the cruelest form of death. God's response to the problem of evil was that He came right down into it, experienced it, and finally, conquered it. Ravi Zacharias said it well: "Suffering and pain did not spare the very Son of God. God conquers not in spite of the dark mystery of evil, but through it."[152]

12. God's Answer: The Cross of Christ

The cross of Christ is God's answer to the problem of suffering and evil. Michael Green eloquently remarks,

> No other faith suggests anything remotely comparable. The cross shows that God is no stranger to pain and evil. God does not allow us to go through what he himself avoids. He came face to face with concentrated evil in this world when he came among us in the person of Jesus... He did not give us an exhaustive answer to the problem of suffering: he shared it.[153]

When I was working as a campus minister at the University of Florida several years ago, I had the great privilege of studying the Bible with a post-graduate Muslim student from Egypt. During one of our discussions about Jesus, I asked him, *"What does the Qur'an say about Jesus?"* He told me that the Qur'an tells us that Jesus was a prophet who was born of a virgin named Mary. He added, "the Qur'an also tells us that Jesus could perform miracles and was without sin." I asked him, *"Why, then, do you not believe that Jesus was "Immanuel" (God with us)?"* His response was interesting. *"Do you know why I can't believe that Jesus was 'God in the flesh?' Because of this..."* He then stood up and spread his arms apart like Jesus on the cross. *"This is weakness! God is God and can't be weak."* I asked him, *"Do you love your children?"* He said, *"Of course, I love my children!"* I asked him, *"At what lengths would you go to show your love for them?"* It seemed that he momentarily forgot the context of our conversation and passionately told me, *"Russ, I would die for my children!"* There was a long silence between us. I eventually spoke, *"You see, that is not weakness. In fact, that is ultimate strength in an act of ultimate love."*

"Only on the cross of Jesus Christ do love, justice and forgiveness converge."

(Ravi Zacharias)

"From the cross there will spring light sufficient to illuminate even the darkest night... A ray of light pierces the gloom ...the impenetrable mystery of evil meets the paradoxical mystery of the cross."

(Henri Blocher)

"For the message of the cross is foolishness to those who are perishing, but to us who are being saved it is the power of God... For the foolishness of God is wiser than man's wisdom, and the weakness of God is stronger than man's strength."

(1 Corinthians 1:18, 25)

13. We are called to be part of the solution of the problem of pain.

In his book entitled, *Where Is God When It Hurts?*, Philip Yancey makes the following insightful comment: "We usually think of the problem of pain as a question we ask of God, but it is also a question he asks of us. How do we respond to hurting people?"[154] Indeed, we see this throughout the Bible. When God spoke to Moses from the burning bush, we find a clear example of how our Creator goes about responding to human suffering. God essentially tells Moses in Exodus 3: "I have heard the cries of my people. I have seen their oppression. Therefore, I am sending you." Likewise, just before Jesus was crucified, He told His disciples, "As the Father has sent me, I am sending you" (John 20:21). He taught His followers that rather than continuing to be a part of the problem of human pain, we should become part of the solution. Throughout the Bible, God's people are called to "defend the cause of the weak and fatherless; maintain the rights of the poor and oppressed. Rescue the weak and needy... Seek justice, encourage the oppressed. Defend the cause of the fatherless, plead the case of the widow" (Psalm 82:3-4; Isaiah 1:17). Furthermore, Christians are reminded in James 1:27 that "religion that God our Father accepts as pure and faultless is this: to look after orphans and widows in their distress and to keep oneself from being polluted by the world." Jesus instructed that in "ministering to the hungry and thirsty, the stranger, the naked, the sick and the prisoner, we would be ministering to him, indicating that he identified himself with all needy and suffering people?"[155]

Conclusion

Human suffering and evil are never the will of God. He may permit it, screen it, even use it for His good purposes, but He is not the cause. Lamentations 3:33 gives us this assurance about God: "He (God) does not willingly bring affliction or grief to the children of men." However, because of His unfathomable love for us, He willingly chose to accept the blame and the punishment for all the evil that humans have ever committed. Let us conclude by hearing these powerful words of John Stott,

"THE LONG SILENCE"
(adapted from John Stott's book "*The Cross of Christ*")

At the end of time, billions of people were scattered on a great plain before God's throne. Most shrank back from the brilliant light before them. But some groups near the front talked heatedly—not with cringing shame, but with belligerence. *"Can God judge us? How can he know about suffering?"* The words came from a thin, starving young girl. She ripped open a sleeve to reveal a tattooed number from a Nazi concentration camp. *"We endured terror...beatings...torture...death!"* In another group, a man lowered the collar on his shirt revealing an ugly rope burn on his neck, *"What about this...I was lynched for no crime, for no reason other than the color of my skin."* All across the plain, there were hundreds of such groups. Each had a complaint against God for the evil and suffering he permitted in the world. *"How lucky God was to live in heaven, where all was sweetness and light... no weeping, no fear, no hunger, no hatred...What did God know of all that humans had been forced to endure in this world?"* —they were saying. So each of these groups sent forth their leader, chosen because he or she had suffered the most—a Jewish person, a black person, a person from Hiroshima, a horribly deformed arthritic, several with various forms of disabilities—at last they were ready to present their case...it was rather clever. They pronounced that before God could be qualified to be their judge, he would have to endure what they had endured. Their decision was... God would have to be sentenced today. Sentenced to live on earth and to live as a man who would suffer. *"Let em' be born a Jew!"* *"Let the legitimacy of his birth be doubted!"* *"Let him know what it is like to be hungry!"* *"Let his work be so difficult that even his family will think he is out of his mind when he tries to do it!"* *"Let him be betrayed by his closest friends!"* *"Let him face false charges!"* *"Let him be tried by a prejudiced jury!"* *"Let him be convicted by a cowardly judge!"* *"Let him be tortured!"* *"Let him see what it means to be so terribly alone and then let him die! Let him die so that there can be no doubt that he died!"* *"Let there be a great host of witnesses to verify it."* As each leader pronounced the portion that he or she would add to the sentence, loud murmurs of approval went up from the throng of people, *"Yes, yes, it's only fair! It's only right!"* *"If he would judge us, he must face what we faced!"* And when the last had finished pronouncing their sentence, **there was a long silence...**

No one dared utter another word. No one could even move. For suddenly, it dawned upon them all. That God had already served his sentence and that God would judge no one in whose shoes he had not already walked in.[156]

If you want to know what God is like... Look at the cross! Jesus, God in the flesh, suffered and died so that you could have forgiveness for your sins, and that you could spend eternity in a place without suffering and evil.

CHAPTER 10

Is There Only One Way to God?

Jesus once told His disciples, "I am the way and the truth and the life. No one comes to the Father except through me."[157] For many in our modern world, His exclusive statement and those who accept it to be absolutely true are seen as arrogant, narrow-minded, and intolerant. We live in a world where many see religious pluralism as the better way, truth as relative, all religions and viewpoints as equally valid, and tolerance as the supreme virtue. A person who dares to make an exclusive truth claim is often vilified and considered offensive. Given that there are so many religions in the world, how can Christians claim that Jesus Christ is the *only* way to God and the *only* hope for humanity? In this chapter, I will seek to address this important question. I will begin by critiquing the claim that "Truth is relative." Then, I will evaluate the view that "All religions are basically saying the same things and are simply different paths to God." Finally, within the next few chapters of this book, I will seek to demonstrate that the question "Is there only one way to God?" can be affirmatively and confidently answered by considering the life, death, and resurrection of Jesus Christ.

What is Truth?

"John Lennon, Pete Townsend and I all had this same thing of rather cobbling together one's own belief system—in my case, one that changes all the time as I need to change it. Because I cannot really come to grips with absolutism… I can't understand how people can be like that. They are exotic creatures to me. How do they get to that place where they know with absolute certainty what's true?"[158] ~ David Bowie

Let us begin by looking at Pontius Pilate's famous question in John 18:38, "What is truth?" Is truth absolute or relative? Are there any universal truths that apply to everyone, at all times, at all places, and in all cultures? These questions are certainly not new. In Plato's *Theaetetus* (written around 369-367 B.C.),[159] the following dialogue between Socrates and Protagoras reveals that relativism is not a new phenomenon. It also serves as perhaps the earliest recorded verbal demonstration that relativism is a self-contradicting position.

Protagoras: Truth is relative. It is only a matter of opinion.

Socrates: You mean that truth is mere subjective opinion?

Protagoras: Exactly. What is true for you is true for you, and what is true for me, is true for me. Truth is subjective.

Socrates: Do you really mean that? That my opinion is true by virtue of it being my opinion?

Protagoras: Indeed I do.

Socrates: My opinion, then, is: Truth is absolute, not opinion, and that you, Mr. Protagoras, are absolutely in error. Since this is my opinion, then you must grant that it is true according to your philosophy.

Protagoras: You are quite correct, Socrates.

Protagoras' propositions sound familiar. Today, the relativistic position on truth, though perhaps more popular, has not become any more coherent. Consider the statement, "All truth is relative." Either the statement itself is relative—which would mean that it is not always true (so why believe it?)—or, the statement is an absolute claim, which would mean that all truth is not relative and would falsify the relativistic position. We can identify the weakness of this viewpoint in the following fictional dialogue:

Relativist:	There is no such thing as truth.
Absolutist:	Is that true? If there is no such thing as truth, then your statement is not true. If it is not true, why should I believe it?
Relativist:	What I'm saying is that there are no absolutes.
Absolutist:	Are you absolutely sure about that?
Relativist:	I'm just saying there are no certainties in life.
Absolutist:	Oh really, are you certain about that?

Over and over again these types of "true for you, not true for me" statements can be shown to be self-refuting. The Christian lecturer, Michael Ramsden summed it up well:

"If someone tells you there is no such thing as truth, they are asking you not to believe them—so don't."[160]

The nature of truth has always been absolutely crucial to the Christian faith. Christianity proclaims that truth is absolute, universal, objective, unchangeable, and embodied in the person of Jesus Christ. This view of truth may seem narrow to many. However, it must be pointed out that all truth claims are exclusive and narrow. Thus, the imperative question should be, "Which truth claims make sense and are correct, verifiable, livable, and relevant to our lives?"

A Critique of Religious Pluralism

We live in a culture where a lot of people treat religion like a potluck dinner. Many journey through life and grab a little from this religion and a little from that, until they end up constructing their own mosaic belief system. You have probably heard someone say things like:

- All religions teach essentially the same things.

- There are several paths to God.

- "The soul of religion is one, but it is encased in a multitude of forms." (Mahatma Gandhi)

- All the great world religions are "like planets that circle around the one absolute truth" and are "different culturally conditioned responses to the Ultimate Real."[161] (John Hick)

- "We [Hindus] accept all religions to be true…the real sin is to call someone else a sinner." (Swami Vivekenanda)

- Isn't it arrogant, narrow-minded and offensive to claim that only one religion has the truth?

Many in our post-modern society subscribe to the bizarre idea that all the world religions are basically teaching the same things. However, nothing could be further from the truth as the following few examples will point out. Christianity, Judaism, and Islam are monotheistic religions believing in only one God. Some Hindus believe that there are 330 million personal gods and goddesses. Many followers of Hinduism, Zen Buddhism and Christian Science are pantheists believing that "all is God." Buddhism is strictly non-theistic and teaches that there is no personal God. "A religion can hardly lead to God," Oxford Professor Alister McGrath reasons, "if it explicitly denies the existence of a god or any gods."[162] In Christianity, "the Word became flesh and made his dwelling among us."[163] In Islam, the Word became the Qur'an and the Christian doctrine of the incarnation is considered blasphemy. The Bible declares that Jesus died on the cross and rose from the dead.[164] The Qur'an teaches that Jesus did not die on a cross.[165] Belief in reincarnation is common to some religions, such as Hinduism and Buddhism. The Bible warns, "man is destined to die once, and after that to face judgment."[166]

The Buddhist scholar, Edward Conze, after reading through a collection of the lives of Roman Catholic saints commented, "there was not one of whom a Buddhist could fully approve… They were bad Buddhists though good Christians."[167]

These examples, and countless others that could be given, demonstrate that it is a ludicrous idea that all religions teach the same things, that they all lead to the same God, or that they are all equally true.[168] Only someone who does not understand the world religions or seeks to distort them to accommodate their pluralistic worldview would make such a claim. Though it is possible that all the world religions could be entirely wrong about God, it is not possible they all could be entirely right. If one religion is true, then logically, the others are false. They can't all be true and contradict one another at the same time. Let us now turn to the issues of arrogance and exclusivity of the Christian truth claims.

Isn't it arrogant to claim that only one religion has the monopoly on truth?

Christianity does not claim that there is no truth in other religions or sacred books. It only claims that Jesus and His Word are true and whatever is contradictory to Jesus and His Word is false. The charge of religious arrogance is often presented in the form of the old Hindu parable of the king, the blind men, and the elephant.

The story is about a king who is watching a group of blind men attempting to figure out what is in front of them, which happens to be an elephant. One man grasps the elephant's tail and claims, "It is obviously a rope." The next man takes hold of the elephant's front leg and suggests, "It is a tree." The third man grabs the elephant's trunk and declares, "You are both wrong, this is unquestionably a large snake!"

The person telling the story is usually suggesting that the followers of the world religions are like the blind men who all had different explanations of a larger reality they could not fully comprehend. Thus, it is implied, it is extremely arrogant for any religious person to claim absolute understanding of "Ultimate Reality." But, hold on. Isn't it condescending for the story-teller to suggest that Jesus, Moses, Muhammad, Buddha, Krishna were all blind, but they—like the wise king in the story—can see the big picture? Isn't it extremely arrogant to imply that all the followers of the great world religions are like ignorant people groping around and clutching onto the little bit of reality they can grasp, while they—the enlightened storyteller—have somehow obtained superior insight on the whole of reality? Again, McGrath writes, "Perhaps a more responsible—and considerably less arrogant—approach would be to suggest that we are all, pluralists included, blind beggars, to whom God graciously makes himself known."[169]

Another popular story that is often used to promote religious pluralism is about a group of hikers, each on a different path, trying to reach the top of a mountain. Each hiker is confident that his path is the only way to get to the summit. However—the storyteller assures us—they are all mistaken because all the different paths eventually lead to the top.

Having been on numerous mountain climbing trips, I would argue that it is extremely foolhardy and dangerous to assume that all paths lead to the summit. Again, isn't it presumptuous to claim that all the faithful adherents to the various world religions are like oblivious mountain climbers, while the storyteller can somehow look down from a privileged, exalted position and see the whole of reality?

So, is it arrogant to claim that Jesus is the only way to God? I would argue that it is no more arrogant to say this than it is to say, "Jesus, Moses, Buddha, Mohammed, Krishna and the billions who follow them are all wrong with their exclusive claims—but I'm right when I claim that all the world religions lead to God."

Another problem with the mountain parable is that it suggests that we must go through an arduous journey to somehow climb our way to God. The Christian faith teaches just the opposite, as Michael Green points out: "The Bible does not record the story of human beings in search of God, but God in search of human beings."[170] In fact, it is significant that the very first question God asks of humanity in the Bible is found in Genesis 3:9: *Where are you?* In the very last book of the Bible, we find the resurrected Jesus continuing to search for and invite us to be where he is:

"Here I am! I stand at the door and knock. If anyone hears my voice and opens the door, I will come in and eat with him, and he with me" (Revelation 3:20). Thus, from Genesis 3 to Revelation 3, we have the story of God's desperate quest to rescue His lost children from death.

Is it wrong to claim you're right?

Some people attack Christians with noble sounding questions such as:

Are we to believe that only the Christians are right and everyone else in the world is wrong? What about good, sincere people of other faiths? Are they going to be eternally condemned? Why can't the holy books from other religions also be from God? How can you be so intolerant to exclude all the other great world religions?

Rabbi Schmuley Boteach (the late Michael Jackson's "spiritual advisor") once expressed these feelings:

> "I am absolutely against any religion that says that one faith is superior to another. I don't see how that is anything different than spiritual racism. It's a way of saying that we are closer to God than you, and that's what leads to hatred."[171]

How are Christians to respond to such attacks? First of all, it is important to point out that truth by definition is exclusive. Any time a truth claim is made, it is implied that anything contrary to that claim is false. Thus, even the statement, "I deny the exclusive nature of truth" turns out to be an exclusive truth claim. Second, Christianity is certainly not the only religion with exclusive truth claims. For example, the Islamic claims are radically exclusive. Hinduism is entirely uncompromising on the law of karma, the authority of the Vedas and reincarnation. Even the Bahá'ís who claim to include everyone, end up excluding the exclusivists (which ironically turns out to be almost everyone).[172]

There are really only four options when it comes to "paths to God."

1) **There is only one way to God.**

2) **All ways lead to God.**

3) **Only some ways lead to God.**

4) **No way leads to God.**

The view that "all roads lead to God" excludes those who say "only one road leads to God" or "only some roads lead to God." The proponents of this seemingly all-inclusive view make the exclusive claim that their view is right and everyone else's is wrong.

Likewise, people who claim "only some ways lead to God" exclude those who believe that option 1, 2 or 4 is correct. Without belaboring the point, we see that all religious claims are exclusive and it is impossible to escape saying that someone else is wrong.

All religions claim to be the *best* option, not just *an* option. Why then should Christians be singled out and called arrogant and exclusive when it turns out that every worldview excludes some and claims that others are wrong? In fact, in predominately Christianized countries, adherents to other religions are free to practice their non-Christian faith. However, when a person chooses to become a follower of Christ in many non-Christianized countries, they are immediately subject to persecution, danger, and violence.

Is Jesus Christ the only way to God? The New Testament answers this question with an emphatic 'Yes!' The apostle Peter is bold, clear and uncompromising in presenting the Christian stance on salvation. In Acts 4:12, he proclaims this about Jesus, "Salvation is found in no one else, for there is no other name under heaven given to men by which we must be saved." The apostle Paul is equally emphatic saying, "there is one God and one mediator between God and men, the man Christ Jesus" (1 Timothy 2:5). If the New Testament is right about this, then we had better follow Jesus. If the New Testament is wrong about this, then Christianity is a false religion and Jesus was a legend, a lunatic,or a fiendish liar. The crucial question should be, 'Which religious claim is correct, verifiably true, and relevant to our lives and how can those claims be defended?' Concerning the Christian faith, C. S. Lewis once wrote, "If it is false, it is of no importance; if true, it is of infinite importance. The one thing it cannot be is moderately important."

In this chapter, I have attempted to show that relativism, religious pluralism, and the idea that "all religions are basically the same" are critically inadequate, unworkable,and ridiculous. I can think of no better illustration of this than Steve Turner's brilliant, satirical poem entitled, *"The Atheist's Creed."*

THE ATHEIST'S CREED
by Steve Turner

We believe in Marxfreudanddarwin.
We believe everything is OK
as long as you don't hurt anyone,
to the best of your definition of hurt,
and to the best of your knowledge.

We believe in sex before, during, and
after marriage.
We believe in the therapy of sin.
We believe that adultery is fun.
We believe that sodomy's OK.
We believe that taboos are taboo.

We believe that everything's getting better
despite evidence to the contrary.
The evidence must be investigated
And you can prove anything with evidence.

We believe there's something in horoscopes

UFO's and bent spoons;
Jesus was a good man just like Buddha,
Mohammed, and ourselves.
He was a good moral teacher although we think
His good morals were bad.

We believe that all religions are basically the same—
at least the one that we read was.
They all believe in love and goodness.
They only differ on matters of creation,
sin, heaven, hell, God, and salvation.

We believe that after death comes Nothing
Because when you ask the dead what happens
they say nothing.
If death is not the end, if the dead have lied, then it's
compulsory heaven for all
excepting perhaps Hitler, Stalin, and Genghis Kahn…

We believe that man is essentially good.
It's only his behavior that lets him down.
This is the fault of society.
Society is the fault of conditions.
Conditions are the fault of society.
We believe that each man must find the truth that
is right for him.
Reality will adapt accordingly.
The universe will readjust.
History will alter.

We believe that there is no absolute truth
excepting the truth
that there is no absolute truth.

We believe in the rejection of creeds,
and the flowering of individual thought.[173]

Steve Turner then adds this sobering post-script called *Chance*:

If chance be the Father of all flesh, disaster is his rainbow in the sky and when you hear State of Emergency! Sniper Kills Ten! ...Bomb Blasts School. It is but the sound of man worshipping his maker.[174]

Do you see what he's saying? He is pointing out that if we choose to live our lives as if everything is o.k., as if we don't really need God, as if all beliefs are equally valid, and as if we can simply make up our own religion, then we should not be too surprised when we hear 'Sniper Kills Ten' or 'Bomb blasts School.' History has shown us time and time again that when humans begin to invent their own rules, morality, reality, truth, and religion, the results are usually grim, tragic, sickening, violent, and dangerous. In his book entitled *The Twilight of Atheism*, Alister McGrath points out "the twentieth century gave rise to one of the greatest and most distressing paradoxes of human history: that the greatest intolerance and violence of that century were practiced by those who believed that religion caused intolerance and violence."[175]

Jesus did not assert, "I am *a* way, *a* truth and *a* life" rather, He claimed, "I am *the* way and *the* truth and *the* life. No one comes to the Father except through me." In the next few chapters, I will seek to demonstrate that this claim is deeply embedded in history, evidence, reason, fact, logic, reality, and personal experience. Unlike any other founder of any other religion, Jesus remarkably backed up His claims by living a sinless life, demonstrating supernatural power, fulfilling ancient prophecy, dying on a cross, and being raised from the dead.

CHAPTER 11

Who Is Jesus?

"Though he was very rich,
yet for your sakes he became poor,
so that by his poverty he could make you rich."
(2 Corinthians 8:9)

The famous cosmetic surgeon, Dr. Maxwell Maltz (1899-1975), tells an amazing story about a woman who visited his office and told him that her husband had been injured in a terrible fire. Sadly, she explained that his face was so disfigured from the burns that he had locked himself in his room and would not let anyone, including her, into his life. Dr. Maltz quickly assured her, "You have come to the right place. We have made tremendous advances in cosmetic surgery and have all the latest technology here in my office. Just tell him to come in…" The woman interrupted, "You don't understand, he will not come. I did not come to ask you to heal him. I have come to ask you to disfigure my face so that he will let me back into his life." Dr. Maltz was utterly amazed. Of course, he did not honor her request. He did, however, go to the man's house to try to convince him to come out. He knocked, but there was silence. Finally, the doctor yelled, "Listen, your wife came to me and begged me to disfigure her so that you would let her back into your life." From behind the walls, he heard weeping. Slowly the door opened, the man came out and entered into a new life. This exemplary wife intended to go to extraordinary measures to identify and connect with her hurting husband to show her love for him.

Have you ever wondered if anyone has this type of love for you?

The Christian faith proclaims the good news that God loves you this way and has proven it by choosing to disfigure Himself in order to identify and connect with our hurting world. The Bible captures this astonishing and attractive thought in these terms:

> "...though he was in the form of God...emptied himself, taking the form of a slave, being born in human likeness. And being found in human form, he humbled himself and became obedient to the point of death—even death on a cross."[176] He had "no beauty or majesty to attract us to him, nothing in his appearance that we should desire him. He was despised and rejected by men, a man of sorrows, and familiar with suffering. Like one from whom men hide their faces he was despised, and we esteemed him not...he was pierced for our transgressions, he was crushed for our iniquities; the punishment that brought us peace was upon him, and by his wounds we are healed."[177]

The Christian faith makes the extraordinary claim that God, Himself visited our world as a full-fledged human being. Spirit became flesh. Infinite became finite. Invisible became visible. The Creator entered His creation. He entered into our world so that we could enter into His world. The King of the Universe became a tiny, vulnerable, peasant child.

One ancient Hebrew prophecy foretells this epic event with these words:

> "Therefore the Lord himself will give you a sign: The virgin will be with child and will give birth to a son, and will call him Immanuel." (Isaiah 7:14 – Immanuel means "God with us.")

What a profound thought! That the only way people on earth could clearly understand what the God of heaven is like was if the God of heaven became a person on earth. That God would enter into our world so that we could enter into His world. Why would God do this? The answer, in a word, is *love*. The 19th century Danish theologian, Søren Kierkegaard put it this way:

"Suppose there was a king who loved a humble maiden. The king was like no other king. Every statesman trembled before his power…and yet this mighty king was melted by love for the humble maiden. How could he declare his love for her? In an odd sort of way, his kingliness tied his hands. If he brought her to the palace and crowned her head with jewels…she would surely not resist—no one dared resist him. But would she love him? She would say she loved him of course, but would she truly?"[178]

This quote from Kierkegaard raises important questions. How could a powerful King declare his love for a humble maiden? How could he show her what he is really like and what really matters to him? How could he win her love? Ah-ha! The King could leave his palace, become a peasant, make his home in the village and live among the common people. This way, the maiden could freely choose to love or ignore the king based on his character.

In 1995, Joan Osbourne released a song entitled "One of Us" in which she asks the question, "What if God was one of us?" Christians believe that a man from a small, Middle Eastern village called Nazareth named Jesus answered this question.

In the next few chapters, we will explore this provocative thought. Specifically, we will focus on the following two questions:

- If God came down to earth in the form of a human being, what would we expect this person to be like?

- Did Jesus of Nazareth display the qualities and characteristics we would expect if He were really God?

You have probably heard the joke about the newly hired doctor walking around the hospital, meeting some of her patients for the first time. She stopped to greet one man and asked his name. The man sat up in his hospital bed and proudly proclaimed, "I am Napoleon Bonaparte—The Emperor of France!" The doctor gently asked, "Oh really, who told you that you were Napoleon Bonaparte?" The patient loudly declared, "God did!" At this point, the man in the bed next to him sat up and yelled, "I DID NOT!"

This humorous story brings up the point that many throughout history have claimed to be a god or a goddess. The question is, "How would someone go about proving a claim like this?" In other words, if God were one of us, how would we know it? What qualities and characteristics would we expect this person to have?

I would like to suggest that we would expect this person to be perfectly good and incredibly powerful. We would expect this person to be able to have a history-changing impact on the world. We would expect this person's words to be the greatest ever spoken. We would expect this person to be able to display supernatural power and to satisfy the spiritual hunger in people's hearts. In the rest of this chapter, we will explore the question, "Did Jesus of Nazareth fulfill these expectations when He lived on earth some two thousand years ago?"

I. If God became a human we would expect that person to be good (without sin).

WAS JESUS OF NAZARETH WITHOUT SIN?

A. Jesus' followers claimed that He was without sin.

The apostles lived and traveled with Jesus for three years. They were with Him every day. If Jesus had any sin in His life, they certainly would have known it.

Peter claimed:

"He committed no sin, and no deceit was found in his mouth." (1 Peter 2:22)

"For Christ died for sins once for all, the righteous for the unrighteous, to bring you to God...." (1 Peter 3:18)

John claimed:

"My dear children, I write this to you so that you will not sin. But if anybody does sin, we have one who speaks to the Father in our defense—Jesus Christ, the Righteous One." (1 John 2:1)

"…You know that he appeared so that he might take away our sins. And in him is no sin." (1 John 3:5)

This is a remarkable claim coming from the apostle John when you consider that Jesus' mother, Mary, lived with him for some time. Apparently, John was the only apostle who was at the cross as Jesus was dying. It is this apostle who records that one of Jesus' last acts of kindness was to make sure His mother had someone to care for her after He was gone. So, as Jesus was hanging on the cross, He said to Mary, **"Dear woman, here is your son,"** and to John He said **"here is your mother."**

John 19:27 tells us, "From that time on, this disciple took her into his home." I find it extremely interesting that later this apostle wrote of Jesus, *"in him is no sin."* Why do I find this interesting? Because Jesus' mother moved in with him! If my mother moved in with you, I can assure you that it would not be long before you heard many stories about the sins of my youth. (If I talked to your mother at length, I bet I could find out something on you, too!)

Paul (who previously was an enemy of Christianity) claimed:

"God made him who had no sin to be sin for us, so that in him we might become the righteousness of God."
(2 Corinthians 5:21)

The writer of the New Testament book of Hebrews claimed:

"For we do not have a high priest who is unable to sympathize with our weaknesses, but we have one who has been tempted in every way, just as we are—yet was without sin." (Hebrews 4:15)

"Such a high priest meets our need—one who is holy, blameless, pure, set apart from sinners, exalted above the heavens." (Hebrews 7:26)

Of course, we would expect His friends to say He was good. What, however, did Jesus' enemies say about him?

B. Jesus' enemies claimed He was without sin.

Interestingly, all the early historical records that we have about Jesus of Nazareth reveal that even His enemies maintained that He was without sin. Consider the following examples:

Judas Iscariot

Judas was a friend, an apostle and a travel companion of Jesus for three years. At the end of these three years, Judas betrayed Jesus for thirty silver coins. If Jesus was a sinner, Judas would have known about it and exposed this to the authorities. This sort of testimony would have completely destroyed Jesus' credibility. However, in the end, Judas could only claim, "I have sinned… for I have betrayed innocent blood" (Matthew 27:4).

The Jewish Leaders

"The chief priests and the whole Sanhedrin were looking for false evidence against Jesus so that they could put him to death. But they did not find any, though many false witnesses came forward…." (Matthew 26:59-60)

Pilate and King Herod

"Pilate called together the chief priests, the rulers and the people, and said to them, 'You brought me this man as one who was inciting the people to rebellion. I have examined him in your presence and have found no basis for your charges against him. Neither has Herod, for he sent him back to us; as you can see, he has done nothing to deserve death.'" (Luke 23:13-15)

A Roman soldier who witnessed the death of Jesus

"The centurion, seeing what had happened, praised God and said, 'Surely this was a righteous man.'" (Luke 23:47)

Pilate's wife

"While Pilate was sitting on the judge's seat, his wife sent him this message: 'Don't have anything to do with that innocent man....'" (Matthew 27:19)

The thief on the cross next to Jesus

"We are punished justly, for we are getting what our deeds deserve. But this man has done nothing wrong." (Luke 23:41)

Jesus even once stood before His enemies and asked them...

"Can any of you prove me guilty of sin?"(John 8:46)

No one could! Jesus' life has always been regarded as the purest in human history. *Time* magazine described His life as "the most persistent symbol of purity, selflessness and brotherly love in the history of man."[179] Even in the religion of Islam, the Qur'an claims that Jesus was without sin.[180] The famous Hindu leader of India, Mahatma Gandhi (1869-1948) described the pure life of Jesus this way, "A man who was completely innocent, offered himself as a sacrifice for the good of others, including his enemies, and became the ransom of the world. It was a perfect act."[181]

II If God became a human, we would expect that person to possess and display supernatural power.

Did Jesus have supernatural power?

Again, we would fully expect Jesus' followers to claim that He had supernatural power. In fact, countless thousands of His followers (from the birth of the Christian Church until today) have chosen to be persecuted, tortured or killed rather than deny their solid conviction and first-hand experience that Jesus of Nazareth possesses supernatural power.

What did the enemies of Jesus say about His miracles?

The earliest historical records we have report that Jesus' enemies expressed the following thoughts about His supernatural power, "'What are we accomplishing?' they asked. 'Here is this man performing many miraculous signs. If we let him go on like this, everyone will believe in him...'" (John 11:47-48) Even early Jewish, Roman, and Islamic writers wrote about Jesus' ability to do miracles. For example, the official records of the Great Sanhedrin ("the supreme court of ancient Israel") reveal that one of the reasons Jesus was crucified was because "he practiced magic."[182] The Roman Emperor, Julian (A.D. 361-363), wrote about Jesus' ability to "heal disabled and blind people and cause demons to leave people."[183] The *Qur'an,* written six hundred years after Jesus walked the earth, speaks of His ability to perform miracles,[184] as well as His virgin birth.[185] Here is a list of some of the miracles of Jesus recorded in the Bible:

Miracles of Jesus Recorded in the Bible

1.	His mother was a virgin when He was born	Matt. 1:18-25; Luke 1:26-38, 2:1-7
2.	He changed water into wine	John 2:1-11
3.	He healed a Roman official's son	John 4:46-54
4.	He healed a man who had an evil spirit	Mark 1:23-28; Luke 4:33-37
5.	He healed Peter's mother-in-law	Matt. 8:15; Mark 1:31; Luke 4:39
6.	He caused many fish to be caught	Luke 5:5-6
7.	He healed a man with leprosy	Matt. 8:2-3; Mark 1:41-42
8.	He healed a man who was paralyzed	Matt. 9:1-8; Mark 2:5; Luke 5:17-26
9.	He healed a man with a disabled hand	Matt. 12:13; Mark 3:5; Luke 6:10
10.	He healed a Roman officer's servant	Matt. 8:13; Luke 7:10

11.	He brought a dead man back to life	Luke 7:11-17
12.	He calmed a stormy sea	Matt. 8:26; Mark 4:39; Luke 8:24
13.	He healed a man with many demons	Matt. 8:32; Mark 5:1-20; Luke 8:33
14.	He healed a woman with internal bleeding	Matt. 9:22; Mark 5:29; Luke 8:44
15.	He gave life to a girl who was dead	Matt. 9:25; Mark 5:42; Luke 8:55
16.	He healed two blind men	Matt. 9:27-31
17.	He healed a man who could not talk	Matt. 9:32-33
18.	He healed a man who was disabled	John 5:1-9
19.	He fed 5,000 people	Mt.14:19; Mk.6:41; Lk.9:16; Jn.6:11
20.	He walked on the sea	Matt. 14:25; Mark 6:48; John 6:19
21.	He healed a girl with an evil spirit	Matt. 15:21-28; Mark 7:24-30
22.	He healed a deaf man	Mark 7:31-35
23.	He fed 4,000 people	Matt. 15:29-39; Mark 8:1-10
24.	He healed a blind man at Bethsaida	Mark 8:22-25
25.	He healed a man who had been born blind	John 9:1-7
26.	He healed a boy with an evil spirit	Matt. 17:18; Mark 9:25; Luke 9:42
27.	Catching a fish with a coin in its mouth	Matt. 17:24-27
28.	He healed a blind man with an evil spirit	Matt. 12:22; Luke 11:14
29.	He healed a woman with an 18-year illness	Luke 13:10-13
30.	He healed a man with a bad disease	Luke 14:1-4
31.	He healed 10 men with leprosy	Luke 17:11-19
32.	He raised Lazarus from the dead	John 11:1-44
33.	He healed a blind man near Jericho	Luke 18:35-43

34. He healed another blind man	Mark 10:46-52
35. He caused a fig tree to dry up	Matt. 21:19; Mark 11:12-21
36. He healed a cut ear	Luke 22:49-51
37. He was resurrected from the dead	Mt. 28; Mk.16; Lk. 24; Jn. 20-21
38. He caused many fish to be caught again	John 21:4-6

The apostle John wrote, **"Jesus did many other miraculous signs in the presence of his disciples, which are not recorded in this book. But these are written that you may believe that Jesus is the Christ, the Son of God, and that by believing you may have life in his name."** (John 20:30-31)

Jesus' miracles demonstrated that He possessed power over nature, evil, demons, sickness, disease, and even death! Again, it is crucial to point out that the New Testament books that record the miracles of Jesus were being circulated while the eyewitnesses of these events were still living. If these miracles did not really happen, someone could have easily said, *"Hold on! I happened to be at the event that this book is talking about and I'm telling you that Jesus did not perform a miracle!"* However, there is no historical record of any eyewitness denying Jesus' power to do miracles.

III If God became a human we would expect this person to have a great and lasting influence on history.

The early historical documentation we have about Jesus is impressive when compared to other important historical figures of the same time period. For example, within the first 150 years after Jesus' death, we have existing evidence of more than forty writers, including nine non-Christian sources, commenting on the life of Jesus.[186] Compare this with the historical documentation we have about Tiberius Caesar, who was the Roman emperor during the time of Jesus. We only have ten existing historical sources that mention Tiberius that date back to the first 150 years of his death.[187] In other words, we have four times the amount of early historical documentation about Jesus than we do for the Roman emperor of that time period!

When Napoleon Bonaparte (1769-1821) was exiled to the island of St. Helena, he expressed these thoughts about the historical impact of Jesus of Nazareth:

> "I know men and I can tell you that Jesus Christ is no mere man. Between him and every other person in the world there is no possible term of comparison. Alexander, Caesar, Charlemagne, and I have founded empires. But on what did we rest the creations of our genius? Upon force. Jesus Christ founded his empire upon love: and at this hour, millions of men and women would die for him." [188]

The positive influence and impact Jesus has had on human history is immeasurable and undeniable. His life literally split history into two halves, as people all around the world measure the date on their calendars from the time of His birth. The fact of the matter is that Jesus has been the most influential, famous, and important person in history for twenty centuries. Today, some two thousand years after His life on earth, He is the center of the largest religion in the world. The church that He founded has become the largest institution in the history of the world. More than two billion people living on earth today call themselves His followers. He is looked upon as a prophet or an "enlightened one" by nearly every major world religion. One unknown writer summarized Jesus' life with these words:

> "Born in an obscure village, he was the child of a peasant woman. Growing up in another out of the way and disdained village, he worked in a carpenter shop until he was about thirty. Then for three years, he was a preacher who both talked and listened. He helped people whenever he could. He never wrote a book. He never held an office. He never went to college. He never had a family of his own or owned a home. He never traveled

over 200 miles from the place where he was born. He never did any of the things that usually accompany greatness and had no credentials but himself. While he was still a young man, the tide of public opinion turned against him. His friends ran away. He was turned over to his enemies. He went through a mockery of a trial, after which he was executed along with two thieves. While he was dying, his executioners gambled for the only piece of property he owned. Only because a generous friend offered his own cemetery plot was there a place for him to be buried.

Two thousand years have now come and gone, and today he is the central figure of the human race. The leader of the column of spiritual progress. The ultimate example of love. It is no exaggeration to say that all the armies that have ever marched, all the navies that ever sailed, all the kings who have ever reigned, all the congresses that have ever convened, put together, have not affected the life of man upon this earth as that One Solitary Life."[189]

IV If God became a human, we would expect that this person's words would be the greatest ever spoken.

History makes it abundantly clear that Jesus was a remarkably gifted teacher. The historian Philip Schaff (1819-1893) once described Jesus' words this way:

"This Jesus of Nazareth, without money and arms, conquered more millions than Alexander, Caesar, Mohammed, and Napoleon; without science and learning, He shed more light on things human and divine than all philosophers and scholars combined; without the eloquence of schools, He spoke such words of life as were never spoken before or since, and produced the effects which lie beyond the reach of orator or poet; without writing a single line, He set more pens in motion, and furnished the themes for more sermons, discussions, learned volumes, works of art and songs of praise than the whole army of great men of ancient and modern times."[190]

Wherever this Jewish rabbi went, large crowds would gather to hear what He had to say. It wasn't just what He said that allured and amazed the crowds, but the way He said it. Jesus spoke with compelling authority. He appeared to teach as if He had been authorized and empowered to speak on God's behalf. He not only seemed to speak *for* God, but *as* God. For example, consider what the Bible says about Jesus' teaching:

"In the past God spoke to our forefathers through the prophets at many times and in various ways, but in these last days he has spoken to us by his Son..." (Hebrews 1:1-2)

"Then he went down to Capernaum, a town in Galilee, and on the Sabbath began to teach the people. **They were amazed at his teaching**, because his message had authority." (Luke 4:31-32)

"Simon Peter answered him, 'Lord, to whom shall we go? **You have the words of eternal life.**'" (John 6:68)

On one occasion, the religious leaders sent the temple guards to arrest Jesus. When the guards returned empty handed, the religious authorities asked them, "Why didn't you bring him in?" Their response was astonishing,

"'**No one ever spoke the way this man does,**' the guards declared." (John 7:45-46)

One writer claims the following about the words of Jesus:

"The Gospels are the greatest literature ever written. They are read by more people, quoted by more authors, translated into more languages, represented in more art, set to more music, than any other book or books written by any man in any century, in any land. Why is this? Because they are the greatest words ever spoken. The words of Jesus deal clearly and authoritatively with the greatest questions and biggest problems in the human heart. Jesus answers questions like:

Who is God? Does He love me? Does He care for me? What should I do to please Him? How does He look at my sin? How can I be forgiven? Where will I go when I die? How must I treat others? No other man can answer these fundamental human questions as Jesus answered them. They are the kind of words and the kind of answers we would expect God to give." [191]

V If God became a human, we would expect this person to fulfill ancient prophecy.

Hundreds of years before the birth of Jesus, the people of Israel recognized that the Hebrew writings (Genesis through Malachi) were the very words of God. Serious students of these Hebrew books understood that God was preparing to send a special person to earth on a rescue mission to liberate people from guilt, sin, and death. This person was called *Messiah* in the Hebrew language, which translates to *Christ* in the Greek language. These words literally mean *the Anointed One.* (In the ancient world, when a man was chosen to be a King, he was anointed by having oil put on his head). The people of Israel anticipated and expected a Messiah. The question was, "How would they know when the Messiah arrived?" The answer: God told the people of Israel what the Messiah would be like long before He was sent. The Old Testament contains more than 300 prophecies about the Messiah.

Here are just a few examples of prophecies about the Messiah in the Old Testament:

1. The Messiah would be a descendant of Abraham, Jacob, Judah, Jesse and King David (Genesis 22:15-18, 49:10; Numbers 24:17; Isaiah 11:1-10; 2 Samuel 7:16; Jeremiah 23:5-6; Isaiah 9:6-7).

2. The Messiah would be the child of a virgin (Isaiah 7:14).

3. The Messiah would be born in the small village of Bethlehem (Micah 5:2).

4. The Messiah would be betrayed by a friend and would be sold for 30 pieces of silver (Zechariah 11:12-13).

5. The Messiah would suffer and die for all people (Isaiah 53).

6. God even told the people of Israel exactly how the Messiah would die (Psalm 22:16; Zechariah 12:10; Isaiah 53).

The people of Israel knew that the Messiah would have to fulfill *all* the prophecies. Otherwise, He could not really be the Messiah that God promised. These prophecies in effect would form a figurative fingerprint that only the true Messiah could match.[192] This gave Israel (and us) a way to rule out imposters and counterfeit Messiahs. These prophecies served to validate the credentials of the true Messiah. Against astronomical odds, Jesus, and only Jesus, matched this prophetic fingerprint.[193] Of all the prophecies and statements about the Messiah in the Old Testament, Jesus fulfilled every single one of them.

We learn from reading the New Testament that Jesus was a descendant of Abraham, Jacob, Judah, Jesse, and King David. His mother was a virgin when He was born and He was born in the small village of Bethlehem. He was later betrayed by His friend for thirty pieces of silver. Jesus suffered and died exactly the way the Old Testament described. In fact, when the prophecies were given about the Messiah being *"pierced"* (Zechariah 12:10; Psalm 22:16), stoning, not crucifixion, was the common method of execution. Crucifixion was not used as a form of execution until much later in history. Isaiah 53:12 says that the Messiah would be *"numbered with the transgressors."* Jesus was, in fact, crucified with two thieves. Psalm 22:18 indicates that the Messiah's garments would be divided and lots would be cast for His clothing. One writer states this about the extraordinary fulfillment of this obscure Old Testament prophecy:

"The hardened, burly soldiers of Rome at the cross centuries later, did not get their Bibles out and say 'Hey, fellows, this is our cue. Here is where we are supposed to fulfill prophecy and gamble for the clothes of Jesus Christ!' Nevertheless, they did! They gambled for his garments (Matthew 27:35). It is doubtful they knew or cared about the prophecy at all, but how significant that men even in unbelief perfectly fulfill the Word of God. It impresses me too, that Psalm 69:21 dares to say centuries in advance that he would be offered gall and vinegar to drink. He was! (Matthew 27:34). Only God could know that, centuries in advance. There are thousands of things he could have been offered. He could have been offered nothing! The prediction that he would be buried in a rich man's tomb, is spectacular (Isaiah 53:9). That simply did not happen to one who died as a criminal. Yet, look at Matthew 27:57-60 and see this 'impossible' fulfillment as Joseph of Arimathaea risked his riches, his reputation, and his life, to claim the body of Jesus to bury in his own unused tomb!"[194]

Professor of Mathematics, Dr. Peter Stoner (Professor Emeritus at Westmont College) in his book entitled *Science Speaks,* decided to determine the mathematical probability that any one man could fulfill just eight of the Old Testament prophecies written about the Messiah. Amazingly, the number came to 1 chance in 10 billion.[195] This is staggering when you realize that Jesus fulfilled 30 Old Testament prophecies about the Messiah (which were written from 500 to 1,000 years before His birth) during the final 24 hours of His life.

The popular Christian author, Max Lucado writes the following: "Did you know that in his life Christ fulfilled 332 distinct prophecies in the Old Testament? What are the mathematical possibilities of all these prophecies being fulfilled in the life of one man?

One chance out of…

840,000,000,000,000,000,000,000
000,000,000,000,000,000,000,000,000,
000,000,000,000,000,000,000,000,000,000,
000,000,000,000,000,000
(That's ninety-seven zeroes!) Amazing!"[196]

Louis Lapides, who grew up in a conservative Jewish home, was astonished when he began to study the prophecies within the Hebrew Scriptures. After becoming a Christian, and later a minister, he expressed the following thought as one of the reasons for his conversion: "The odds alone say it would be impossible for anyone to fulfill the Old Testament prophecies. Yet Jesus—and only Jesus throughout all of history—managed to do it."[197]

Jesus Christ is the only figure in history whose birth, life, and death were predicted and described hundreds of years before He was born.

> *"Everything that is written by the prophets*
> *about the Son of Man will be fulfilled."*
> **(Luke 18:31)**

VI If God became a human, we would expect this person to satisfy the spiritual hunger in people's hearts.

In every human heart, there is a hunger and thirst that nothing on this earth ever seems to satisfy. Remarkably, Jesus had the audacity to profess that He, and He alone, could satisfy our spiritual hunger and thirst. He maintained that He could fill the "God-shaped void" in our hearts and souls.

To those who were spiritually hungry, Jesus declared,

"I am the bread of life. He who comes to me will never go hungry, and he who believes in me will never be thirsty." (John 6:35)

To those battling depression, despair, and darkness, Jesus claimed,

"I am the light of the world. Whoever follows me will never walk in darkness, but will have the light of life." (John 8:12)

To those who were fearful of death, Jesus boldly proclaimed,

"I am the resurrection and the life. He who believes in me will live, even though he dies; and whoever lives and believes in me will never die." (John 11:25)

To those desperately searching for some kind of spiritual reality, absolute truth, direction, meaning and value system, Jesus said,

"I am the way and the truth and the life." (John 14:6)

To those weighed down by worry, anxiety, fear, shame and guilt, Jesus invited,

> "Come to me, all you who are weary and burdened, and I will give you rest. Take my yoke upon you and learn from me, for I am gentle and humble in heart, and you will find rest for your souls." (Matthew 11:28)

To those who were thirsty to find something more out of life, Jesus stated,

> "If anyone is thirsty, let him come to me and drink. Whoever believes in me, as the Scripture has said, streams of living water will flow from within him." (John 7:37-38)

To those who were simply bored, dissatisfied and disillusioned with life,

> Jesus declared, "I have come that they may have life, and have it to the full." (John 10:10)

Over and over again, Jesus presented Himself as the answer to our deepest needs and desires. These were (and still are) bold and audacious claims. Were these assertions the ravings of an eccentric madman? Were they the claims of a devilish liar? Or, could they be true? When Bono, the lead singer of U2, was asked if the claim of Jesus' divinity was farfetched, he responded this way:

> No, it's not farfetched to me. Look, the secular response to the Christ story always goes like this: he was a great prophet, obviously a very interesting guy, had a lot to say along the lines of other great prophets, be they Elijah, Muhammad, Buddha, or Confucius. But actually Christ doesn't allow you that. He doesn't let you off that hook. Christ says: No. I'm not saying I'm a teacher. Don't call me teacher. I'm not saying I'm a prophet. I'm saying: "I'm the Messiah." I'm saying: "I am God incarnate." And people say: No, no, please, just be a prophet. A prophet, we can take... But don't mention the "M" word! Because, you know, we're gonna have to crucify you. And he goes: No, no. I know you're expecting me to come back with an army, and set you free from these creeps, but actually I am the Messiah... So what you're left

with is: either Christ was who he said he was—the Messiah—or a complete nutcase... The idea that the entire course of civilization for over half of the globe could have its fate changed and turned upside-down by a nutcase, for me, that's farfetched.[198]

Billions and billions of people all over the world would agree because they have experienced that only Jesus Christ can satisfy a person's spiritual hunger and quench a person's spiritual thirst.

Let us end this chapter about Jesus of Nazareth with the striking conclusion of C. S. Lewis:

"A man who was merely a man and said the sort of things Jesus said would not be a great moral teacher. He would either be a lunatic—on a level with the man who says he is a poached egg—or else he would be the devil of hell. You must make your choice. Either this man was, and is, the Son of God or else a madman or something worse... But let us not come with any patronizing nonsense about him being a great human teacher. He has not left that open to us. He didn't intend to. We are faced, then, with a frightening alternative. This man we are talking about either was (and is) just what he said or else a lunatic, or something worse. Now it seems to me obvious that he was neither a lunatic nor fiend and consequently, however strange or terrifying or unlikely it may seem, I have to accept the view that he was and is God. God has landed on this enemy-occupied world in human form." [199]

CHAPTER 12

Was Jesus Really Raised From the Dead?

"I am the resurrection... Do you believe this?"
~ **Jesus Christ**

J. M. Barrie's famous character, Peter Pan (the boy who refused to grow up), once declared, "To die will be an awfully big adventure!" Most of us, however, have a less optimistic view of death and would be more inclined to agree with Woody Allen who once said, "It's not that I'm afraid to die, I just don't want to be there when it happens." I recently read a humorous book in which the author (an American who has lived in England most of her life) contrasted the vastly different ways British people and North Americans view aging and death. Here are some of the observations presented in this book.[200]

> **The British outlook on aging and death:** The British roll
> with the punches. It's fruitless to attempt to outwit destiny.
> People should not try too hard to hold back the ravages of
> time. Face-lifts and jogging geriatrics are vaguely obscene.
> One should grow old gracefully and bow to the inevitable (be
> content to look dreadful). Any Brit over sixty-five, regardless
> of financial circumstances, rejoices in the title of "old-age
> pensioner." The label is designed to depress him to death
> quickly, thus saving money for the State. The financial
> arrangements made for them by the State are predicated
> on the idea that, as you get older, your system slows down,
> so you don't need to eat. Many impoverished OAP's (old

age pensioners) have the decency to retreat to damp and gloomy basement flats where no one sees them (until a caring milkman, alerted by souring pints on the doorstep, pronounces them dead).

The American outlook on aging and death: The single most important thing to know about Americans—the attitude which truly distinguishes them from the British—is that Americans think that death is optional. They may not admit it, but it is a state of mind, that colors everything they do. There's a nagging suspicion that you can delay death (or—who knows? —avoid it altogether) if you really try. This explains the common preoccupation with heath, aerobics, and plastic surgery. The idea is that you're given one life to live, and it's up to you to get it right. If this means facelifts or eye-lid surgery or hair transplants…go for it. If it means a new BMW, which simply makes you *feel* as if you'll live longer, then that's okay, too. You should use the time to maximize individual potential (have a nose job, get a college degree) so as to ensure the highest quality life possible. That's the secret of America's fundamental optimism. You owe it to yourself to be beautiful, clever, skinny, successful, and healthy. If you fail, it's because you're not trying hard enough (you didn't jog regularly, you should've eaten more bran). Death becomes your fault.

However a culture or an individual chooses to approach the issue of death, the ominous and ultimate statistic still remains—one out of every one dies. During the sixteenth and seventeenth centuries, Dutch artists, who had been commissioned to paint pleasant, upbeat scenes for the wealthy, would often insert some object in their paintings that would serve to remind the well-to-do art collectors of their own mortality, the brevity of life, the fleetingness of earthly pleasures and the certainty of death. Hidden somewhere in an otherwise cheerful scene, the artist might place something as subtle as a flower losing its petals, a rotting piece of fruit, an hourglass, an extinguished candle, a clock decorated with the Latin phrase *"ultima forsan"* (which means "perhaps the last [hour]") or something as obvious as a skull or the Latin phrase *"Memento mori"* (which means "Remember you will die").[201] These artists were sending a message, a stark reminder to the affluent: Death is a reality that we may attempt to evade, but we will not be able to avoid. The problem with life is that death always seems to have the last word. Wouldn't it be great if there was someone, somewhere, who had the last word over death?

The good news and unique message of the Christian faith is that there *is* Someone who has the last word over death. Death has been ultimately defeated by Jesus Christ! In John 11:25-26, Jesus made this astonishing declaration:

> "I am the resurrection and the life. He who believes in me will live, even though he dies; and whoever lives and believes in me will never die. Do you believe this?"

What a statement! How could anyone take a proclamation like this seriously? Why in the world would anyone believe this? The answer is this: The reason we can take this statement seriously is that there is overwhelming historical evidence that shortly after Jesus was unquestionably killed on a cross, He appeared to a large number of people, and they clearly saw Him alive. Just around twenty-five years after Jesus was publicly crucified, a letter, written by a former enemy of the Christian faith, was being widely circulated making the incredible claim that Jesus was alive and had been seen by more than five hundred people, including the author of the letter himself. In this famous letter (written around A.D. 55),[202] the apostle Paul wrote the following:

> "For what I received I passed on to you as of first importance: that Christ died for our sins according to the Scriptures, that he was buried, that he was raised on the third day according to the Scriptures, and that he appeared to Peter, and then to

the Twelve. After that, he appeared to more than five hundred of the brothers at the same time, most of whom are still living, though some have fallen asleep. Then he appeared to James, then to all the apostles, and last of all he appeared to me also, as to one abnormally born." (1 Corinthians 15:3-8)

In these verses, Paul tells us three things about the Christian faith that are "of first importance:"

1) **Jesus Christ died for our sins.**

2) **He was buried.**

3) **He was raised from the dead and appeared to a multitude of witnesses.**

It is hard to overstate the importance and the implications of the resurrection of Jesus for the Christian faith and for all of humanity. Paul put it in these terms, "...if Christ has not been raised, our preaching is useless and so is your faith. More than that, we are then found to be false witnesses about God, for we have testified about God that he raised Christ from the dead... And if Christ has not been raised, your faith is futile; you are still in your sins. Then those also who have fallen asleep in Christ are lost. If only for this life we have hope in Christ, we are to be pitied more than all men."[203] In other words, all of Christianity stands or falls with the resurrection.

If Jesus Christ was not raised from the dead...

- The Christian faith is useless and futile.

- A Christian is a false witness and thus, an enemy of God.

- Every Christian, either alive or dead, is lost and still in their sins.

- Jesus was either a fraud or a lunatic.

- Jesus' power was limited and His testimony was a lie.

- We should not believe that any of the miracles in the Bible actually occurred.

- Everything in the New Testament and everything Jesus said should be held suspect.
- The Bible is not true and Christianity is a false religion.

If Jesus Christ was raised from the dead...

- Jesus' power is unlimited.
- Everything Jesus said should be believed and followed.
- Eternal life is both possible and available.
- The truth of biblical Christianity is confirmed.
- We can be assured of God's existence, love, and power.
- Christians can be sure that their sins are forgiven and that they will be raised from the dead to be with God forever in heaven.
- All other religions are false religions.

So, we see that the stakes couldn't be higher. Christians are betting their eternal destiny on the fact that a Jerusalem tomb was empty because God raised Jesus from the dead. In the next two chapters, we will examine these important questions:

Was Jesus really raised from the dead or did something else happen to His body?

Is there enough credible evidence for a rational person to conclude that Jesus' resurrection was a real event in history?[204]

Dr. Simon Greenleaf was one of the greatest legal minds in the history of the U.S. He was named as the Royall Professor of Law at Harvard Law School in 1833. After twenty years of teaching law at Harvard, he completed a three-volume work called *A Treatise on the Law of Evidence,* and it remained a standard textbook in American law throughout the nineteenth century. Dr. Greenleaf was a skeptic of Christianity and would frequently mock and put down Christians in his law classes at Harvard. One year, some of the Christian students in the law program got tired of the ridicule and challenged Dr. Greenleaf to apply his expertise and the principles found in his three volumes on the laws of legal evidence to the evidence for the resurrection of Christ. After much persuasion, he finally accepted the challenge and began to apply his own principles of evaluating evidence to the resurrection. In the process, he became a believer and eventually concluded that the resurrection of Jesus Christ is one of the best-established facts of history according to the laws of legal evidence administered in the courts of justice. What changed his mind? What evidence did he, and so many others, discover to change their thinking on this issue?

A simple starting point: Historical cause and effect

Imagine that you live in the year A.D. 5,000. You are a historian and an archeologist. You are trying to find out what happened historically during the 20th century. During one of your archeological digs, you discover a territorial map of Europe from 1942.

Ah-ha! Now you know that in the early 1940s someone named Hitler was either a king or some other sort of ruler, and he ruled most of Europe. Then, later as you continue your archeological research, you find a map dated 1948. Interestingly, this map has no mention of Hitler and shows that Germany had been split into two parts. From this map, you learn that by 1948 West Germany was aided by Great Britain, the U.S., and France while East Germany was under Soviet control. From the information on these two maps, you have the following facts:

—————————————————] ? [———————————————

Hitler dominated Europe in 1942   1948 – Germany is a defeated, split nation

Just using this information, as a logical historian, what would you assume happened in this time gap? I think it would be safe to assume that something monumental and profound happened between 1942 and 1948. Now, let us carry this same logic over and look at the beginnings of Christianity.

Consider the historical information we have about the year in which Jesus was killed.[205]

————————————————] ? [————————————————

Friday, Passover Time, A.D. 33 -	[— Pentecost, A.D. 33 - (50 days later)
No Christian Church exists	[— The Christian Church has 3,000 members
Jesus hangs dead on a cross	[— Peter boldly preaches that Jesus is alive
Peter denies even knowing Jesus	[— Saul, enemy of Christianity, converts
Jesus' followers have deserted Him	[— James becomes leader of Jerusalem church
Judas betrayed Him and hangs himself	[— All apostles (but John) and others martyred because of their message that Jesus is alive
Women followers are crying and mourning	[— A.D. 150 Christianity spreads over the Roman world
Jesus' brothers do not even believe in Him	[— A.D. 330 Roman Empire supports Christianity
(This is not a very promising start of a world religion, is it?)	[— A.D. 450 Rome Falls/Europe Christianized

I think it is safe to say that something radical, monumental, and profound happened in history between Jesus' crucifixion and Pentecost.[206] Something extraordinary clearly occurred and demands an explanation. What happened? What caused a history-changing religion to pop up out of nowhere? C.F.D. Moule, the esteemed Cambridge University New Testament scholar, put it this way:

"If the coming into existence of the [church], a phenomenon undeniably attested by the New Testament, rips a great hole in history, a hole the size and shape of Resurrection, what does the secular historian propose to stop it up with?" [207]

What Happened to the Body of Jesus?

In addressing this crucially important question, let us begin by considering only the data that virtually all ancient historians and scholars (whether Christian, non-Christian, or skeptic) agree on. The following data are "so strongly evidenced historically that nearly every scholar regards them as reliable facts." [208]

1) A man named Jesus lived and He died by crucifixion on a Roman cross.

2) Jesus was buried in a tomb.

3) On the Sunday morning following Jesus' crucifixion, the tomb was empty.

4) The disciples of Jesus believed that He appeared to them risen from the dead.

5) This belief dramatically changed the disciples.

6) The early church preached the message that Jesus was alive.

7) This message was first proclaimed in Jerusalem.

8) The early Christians worshiped on Sunday.

9) Paul, a former enemy and persecutor of Christians, suddenly became a leader within the early Christian church.

10) James, the skeptical, unbelieving brother of Jesus, suddenly changed and became a leader within the early Christian church in Jerusalem.

These facts are heavily attested and historically supportable even if the Bible is not used as a source of evidence. Thus, the following questions emerge: "How do we explain and interpret these agreed upon historical facts?" "What explanation best accounts for these facts?" "Are there plausible rival theories (other than the traditional resurrection story) that might account for these facts?" Over the centuries, several rival theories have been developed and put forth that attempt to explain these historical facts. Let's take a look at these opposing theories and see if they appear to be plausible:

"Maybe Jesus never really died and somehow He escaped from the tomb."

The early historical documentation we have that Jesus really died by crucifixion is extremely compelling. For example, the crucifixion of Jesus is recorded by the first century Jewish historian Josephus,[209] by Tacitus[210] (who is considered the greatest Roman historian from antiquity) around A.D. 115, by the Greek satirist, Lucian[211] in the mid-second century, by the first century Syrian writer, Mara Bar–Serapion,[212] and the death of Jesus is even recorded in the Jewish Talmud.[213] It is important to note that these are all early non-biblical, non-Christian sources.

Problems with this theory:

1) Jesus was flogged (Matthew 27:26; Mark 15:15; John 19:1). The third-century church historian, Eusebius of Caesarea wrote the following about the horrors of a Roman scourging: "the sufferer's veins were laid bare, and the very muscles, sinews, and bowels of the victim were open to exposure."[214] Another historian wrote that when a man was scourged under the Roman law, "he was bound in a kneeling position so that his naked back was exposed. The lash was a long, leather thong

studded at intervals with pieces of sharp bone, lead and rocks which literally tore a man's back into strips. Many a man had died under the lash; still more had lost their reason and emerged raving mad; few retained consciousness to the end of that bitter ordeal; and all who survived were broken men."

2) Jesus was nailed to a cross. (Matthew 27; Mark 15; Luke 23; John 19). Leon Morris in his commentary on the Gospel of John writes the following about the Roman practice of crucifixion:

> "Nothing could be more horrible than the sight of this living body, breathing, seeing, hearing, still able to feel and yet reduced to the state of a corpse by forced immobility and absolute helplessness. We cannot even say that the crucified person writhed in agony, for it was impossible for him to move. Stripped of his clothing, unable even to brush away the flies which fell upon his wounded flesh, already lacerated by the preliminary scourging, exposed to the insults and curses of people who can always find some sickening pleasure in the sight of the tortures of others. A feeling which is increased and not diminished by the sight of pain—the cross represented miserable humanity reduced to the last degree of impotence and suffering. The penalty of crucifixion combined all that the ardent tormentor could desire, torture, degradation, and certain death, distilled slowly drop by drop."[215]

3) John 19:34 tells us that one of the Roman soldiers "pierced Jesus' side with a spear, bringing a sudden flow of blood and water."[216] In the March 21, 1986 issue of *Journal of the American Medical Association*, a team of three medical experts, including a pathologist from Mayo Clinic, studied the ancient Roman procedures of scourging and crucifixion and their affects on the victim. They made it clear in this article that blood and water would not have come out unless the body was, in fact, dead. The blood and water were due to the rupturing of the sac surrounding the heart (called the pericardium). The medical team quoted in the *JAMA* article concluded, "clearly, the weight

of the historical and medical evidence indicates that Jesus was dead before the wound to his side was inflicted. Accordingly, interpretations based on the assumption that Jesus did not die on the cross appear to be at odds with modern medical knowledge."[217] John, the first-century apostle/fisherman, certainly was no expert in pathology and did not understand all the medical reasons this happened. He was simply reporting what he saw. This, by the way, is strong evidence that John's description of the crucifixion was an eyewitness account.

4) The Roman soldiers were convinced that Jesus was dead, thus "they did not break his legs." (John 19:31-33)

5) Pilate (the Roman governor) was convinced by the Roman centurion that Jesus was dead, so he gave Joseph permission to remove the body from the cross (Mark 15:44-45). Furthermore, the Roman law did not allow anyone to remove someone's body from a cross until the death of that individual was obvious and certain.

6) The Jewish leaders wanted guards at the tomb because they were afraid that the disciples would try to steal the body. This is evidence that the Jewish leaders believed that Jesus was dead (Matthew 27:62-66).

7) Even if the beaten, mutilated, scourged, and pierced Jesus did survive the cross and somehow managed to escape from the tomb, when He appeared to His disciples in this feeble, hurting condition, they would hardly be convinced that He was the risen Prince of Life. Gary Habermas points out that upon seeing their barely alive master "limping, bleeding, pale, and stooped over in pain, Peter would not have responded, 'Wow, I can't wait to have a resurrection body just like that!' Rather the disciples would have said, 'Let's get you a doctor. You need help!'"[218]

"Maybe the disciples stole the body."

The gospel of Matthew tells us that the Jewish leaders gave the Roman soldiers money and told them to say that the disciples had stolen the body of Jesus (Matthew 28:11-15). We find in the writings of Justin Martyr (*Dialogue with Trypho*–A.D. 150) that the Jewish leaders were continuing to spread this rumor in his day. However, there are many fatal problems with this theory.

1) The soldiers claimed that Jesus' followers stole the body. They also said that they were asleep when the theft occurred (Matthew 28:12-13). Does this sound fishy? How would they know who stole the body if they were asleep?

2) We learn in Matthew's Gospel that the body of Jesus was placed in a rock tomb, an incredibly heavy stone was rolled across the entrance, and Roman guards were placed outside the tomb (Matthew 27:59-66). Historians tell us that if a Roman soldier fell asleep while on guard duty, he would be executed [219] and that there were usually at least four men in a Roman guard unit.[220] Is it possible that all of the guards, fully aware that they would be executed if they dozed off, fell asleep at the same time? Is it possible that a huge stone was rolled away from the entrance of the tomb and this sound did not wake anyone up?

3) If the disciples stole the body of Jesus from the tomb, sooner or later someone who knew the facts would have talked. People do not knowingly die for lies. All of the apostles (except John) were killed because they taught that Jesus was raised from the dead. Is it likely that they would have persisted with this lie all the way to their death?

4) Matthew 27:65-66 tells us that the Roman soldiers sealed the tomb. The sealing was always done in the presence of the Roman guards who were left in charge to protect this stamp of Roman authority and power. The followers of Jesus would

have been severely punished for breaking the Roman seal.

Albert Roper notes the following about the Roman guards:

> "Their sole purpose and obligation that evening was to rigidly perform their duty as soldiers of the empire of Rome to which they had dedicated their allegiance. The Roman seal affixed to the stone before Joseph's tomb was far more sacred to them than all the philosophy of Israel or the sanctity of her ancient creed. Soldiers cold blooded enough to gamble over a dying victim's cloak are not the kind of men to be hoodwinked by timid Galileans or to jeopardize their Roman necks by sleeping on their post." [221]

5) The authorities never issued an arrest warrant for the disciples. They never explained how the disciples could have possibly stolen the body or insisted that they produce the body. The authorities knew better than anyone that the disciples did not have the body.

6) If the disciples (or anyone else for that matter) decided to sneak past the Roman guards, roll away the large stone and steal the body, why would they take the time to remove and fold the grave clothes? Merrill Tenney explains the customary Jewish grave clothes as follows:

> "In preparing a body for burial according to Jewish custom, it was usually washed and straightened, and then bandaged tightly from the armpits to the ankles in strips of linen about a foot wide. Aromatic spices often of a gummy consistency, were placed between the wrappings or folds. They served partially as a preservative and partially as a cement to glue the cloth wrappings into a solid covering. John's Gospel tells us that some seventy pounds of spices were used in this process (John 19:38-42)—thus, the grave clothes would not easily be removed. On the morning of the first day of the week the body of Jesus had vanished, but the grave clothes were still there (John 20:5-9)." [222]

7) If the disciples stole the body, this means that the writers of the New Testament would have had to invent a story about Jesus being raised from the dead. According to the New Testament, the first people to find that the tomb was empty and to encounter the risen Jesus were women. If the writers simply made up this story, it would have been unlikely that they would have chosen women as the primary witnesses to the resurrection. This would have certainly hurt the credibility of their story. Unfortunately, in the first century, a women's testimony meant nothing in the Jewish and Roman cultures. Women were not even allowed to give evidence in Jewish courts of law in the first century. For example, consider the following early Jewish writings: "Any evidence which a woman [gives] is not valid..." (Talmud, Rosh Hashannah 1.8)

> "But let not the testimony of women be admitted, on account of the levity and boldness of their gender..." (Josephus, *Antiquities* 4.8.15)

I'm not exactly sure what Josephus meant by that, but it certainly shows the attitude of the day. If the account of the empty tomb had merely been invented by the disciples, it seems extremely unlikely that they would have chosen women to be the primary witnesses. It seems far more likely that they would have chosen men as the first to see the risen Jesus.

8) If the disciples said to themselves, "Hey, Jesus said He would be raised from the dead. We better do something to save face!" The easiest way to go about this would be to claim that Jesus was "spiritually resurrected." How would anyone falsify that claim? Instead, however, they taught about the resurrection of the actual physical body of Jesus.

"Maybe the body was removed by Jesus' enemies."

Problems with this theory:

1) Jesus' enemies had no reason or motive to remove the body. They would have had absolutely nothing to gain by doing this.

2) The enemies of Jesus wanted the body to stay in the tomb. That is why they asked Pilate to put Roman guards around the entrance (Matthew 27:62–28:14).

3) Pilate took great precaution to make sure the body remained in the tomb.

4) The enemies of Jesus never claimed they removed the body from the tomb. They claimed instead that the disciples stole the body.

5) If the enemies stole the body of Jesus, they would have admitted it and could have produced the decaying body with dramatic effect when the apostles started telling people that Jesus was raised from the dead. This would have humiliated the apostles, proved that they were lying, and silenced their resurrection claims forever.

"Maybe the women and disciples looked in the wrong tomb."

Problems with this theory:

1) If the women and disciples went to the wrong tomb, the Roman and Jewish authorities could have easily gone to the right tomb and produced the body, which would have stopped Christianity in its tracks.

2) Even if some of the disciples had gone to the wrong tomb, this would not account for their firm belief that they had encountered the risen Jesus. It was not the empty tomb that convinced the disciples that Jesus was alive; it was the post-crucifixion appearances.

3) These women had carefully noted where the body of Jesus was buried less than 40 hours before.

> "The women who had come with Jesus from Galilee followed Joseph and saw the tomb and how his body was laid in it."
> (Luke 23:55)

4) How did Jesus' grave clothes get in the wrong tomb? We learn in John's Gospel that when the disciples looked in the tomb, the body of Jesus had disappeared, but His grave clothes were still there (John 20:5-9).

5) The evidence suggests that the location of the tomb was well-known because it belonged to Joseph of Arimathea, a recognized public figure, a member of the Jewish Sanhedrin and a "prominent member of the Council" (Mark 15:43).

"Maybe the resurrection story is simply a legend that developed over time after Jesus' death."

Problems with this theory:

1) The resurrection story can be traced back to the eyewitness experiences of the original apostles and the writers of the New Testament. It is well-accepted (even among skeptical critics) that all four Gospels (Matthew, Mark, Luke, and John) attest to the resurrection of Jesus and were written during the first century. In fact, some of Paul's accounts of the resurrection story can be traced back to just a few years after the crucifixion. For example, consider the information found in 1 Corinthians 15:1-8. The combination of archaeology and ancient non-biblical manuscripts help date Paul's letter to the Corinthians between two historical parameters.

The beginning parameter would be A.D. 51. Acts 18:12 mentions that Paul's initial visit to Corinth occurred while

"Gallio was proconsul of Achaia." Archaeologists have unearthed an inscription found at Delphi, Greece, which records that Gallio's proconsulship in the province of Achaia took place in A.D. 51-52. When reading 1 Corinthians it becomes obvious that this letter was written after his initial visit.

The ending parameter would be the year A.D. 68, because we know from several early non-biblical writers that Paul was beheaded during the persecution of Christians instigated by the Roman Emperor Nero (who reigned between A.D. 54 and 68).[223] Most New Testament scholars date the writing of 1 Corinthians around A.D. 54 and believe that Paul was quoting an already-established, early Christian creed in chapter 15. There are several indicators that this creed predates the writings of Paul and serves as one of the earliest Christian teachings available.[224] The fact that this creed lists numerous appearances of the risen Jesus helps us to defuse allegations from critics that the "resurrection story" was simply a legend that slowly developed long after Jesus' death. The appearance of this creed in 1 Corinthians 15 shows that the resurrection of Jesus was part of the earliest Christian traditions and teachings.

2) The legend theory can't explain the empty tomb. All the writings from the time period of Jesus' death show that the tomb was empty, and there is no other early burial tradition in existence.

3) The legend theory can't account for the early evidence that Paul, originally an enemy of the Christian faith, became a faithful follower of Christ based on his firm belief that he had personally encountered the risen Jesus. We will discuss more about Paul's conversion in the next chapter.

4) The legend theory can't explain the remarkable change in the original apostles' lives.

As early as 50 days after Jesus' death, we have abundant evidence that the original disciples were willing to suffer extreme persecution and even martyrdom for their claims that Jesus had personally appeared to them alive after being crucified. This indicates that they firmly believed that what they were claiming about the resurrection really happened. The fact that the original apostles' were radically transformed by the resurrection of Christ is well-documented by early non-biblical writers and serves as compelling evidence that the resurrection story was not embellished over time.[225]

5) In a letter written to the church in Philippi, Polycarp (c. A.D. 69– c. A.D. 155), a contemporary and student of the apostles, who was martyred for his faith in Smyrna (modern Izmir, Turkey) mentions the resurrection of Jesus five times.[226] This letter to the Philippian church was written around A.D. 110. This is further early evidence that the resurrection story was not slowly developed and embellished over a long period of time, but rather can be traced to the original eyewitnesses.

In the next chapter, we will continue looking at the rival theories and will see that all the opposing theories that have developed over the centuries fail to adequately account for the collection of historical facts and early evidence we have.

CHAPTER 13

How Do We Know the Resurrection Occurred?

*"Is there any meaning in my life that
the inevitable death awaiting me does not destroy?"*
~ Leo Tolstoy (1828-1910)

*"Jesus is the first fruits, the pioneer of life.
He has forced open a door that has been locked
since the death of the first man.
He has met, fought, and beaten the King of Death.
Everything is different because he has done so.
This is the beginning of the new creation
and a new chapter in cosmic history has opened."* [227]
~ C. S. Lewis (1898-1963)

In the last chapter, we began looking at the most important and greatest event in human history—the resurrection of Jesus Christ. There are two relevant questions when it comes to the resurrection of Jesus Christ. First, "Did it really happen?" and second, "So what?—If it did really happen, what difference does it make?" In this chapter, we will continue to consider these crucial questions. Let's begin by looking at how the Islamic faith addresses the resurrection of Jesus.

The Qur'an makes the assertion that Jesus was not actually killed on the cross, saying, "they did not slay him, neither crucified him, only a likeness of that was shown to them... God raised him up to Him." (Qur'an, Surah 4:156-158).[228] The original Arabic text is interpreted in different ways within Islam. Some

Muslim scholars interpret this verse to say that when the mob came to arrest Jesus, God made someone else, perhaps Judas, look like him. In other words, God substituted Judas with Jesus, the mob arrested Judas instead, and the betrayer, not Jesus, died on the cross. This view of the crucifixion, however, is plagued with problems.

1) First of all, there are no early Greek, Roman, Jewish, Christian or non-Christian historians or writers who would agree with this assertion. In other words, every early non-Islamic historian would disagree with this view. Who are we going to trust—the eyewitnesses and the writers who lived close to the time of Jesus' death or a document written over six centuries after the event?

2) This view would not explain the empty tomb, the disciples' profound conviction that they had seen the risen Jesus, or the mysterious nature of the resurrection appearances. Jesus is said to have suddenly appeared behind locked doors (John 20:19) and would suddenly disappear from people's sight (Luke 24:31).

3) This view would imply that God and Jesus were involved in fraud and deception, which goes against what the Bible and the Qur'an say about their holy characters.

4) This seventh-century theory would contradict two separate first-century accounts of the suicide of Judas (Matthew 27: 3-10 and Acts 1:18). Again, who is the more reliable historian —Matthew, the first-century eye-witness, or Mohammed, who lived centuries later?

5) If Judas (or anyone else, for that matter) was being crucified in place of Jesus, the victim would have loudly protested this action. Yet, no such protests are recorded by the eyewitnesses.

6) Finally, even several leading Islamic scholars reject this theory of Jesus' death. For example, Dr. Kamel Hussein has said the

following: "The idea of a substitute for Christ is a very crude way of explaining the Qur'anic text... No cultured Muslim believes it nowadays."[229]

"Maybe the 'resurrected Jesus' was really just a vision or a hallucination."

Problems with this theory:

1) Hallucinations do not explain the empty tomb.

2) One of the earliest traditions of the Christian church is that the disciples of Jesus saw the risen Christ as a group. Paul tells us in 1 Corinthians 15:7 that over five hundred people saw the risen Christ at one time. Hallucinations are not group experiences. They are like dreams, in that, they are experienced only by individuals.

3) The disciples in the New Testament claim that they ate with Jesus and touched Him after He was resurrected.

4) Finally, this theory (and all the other rival theories) can't adequately explain what happened to a man named Saul.

Who was Saul?

Saul was an enemy of the early Christian church who sincerely believed that it was God's will to stop Jesus' followers from promoting their message of a resurrected Messiah. He described his early life with these words: "For you have heard of my previous way of life in Judaism, how intensely I persecuted the church of God and tried to destroy it" (Galatians 1:13). Saul was in the crowd, giving his approval, when a young Christian named Stephen was stoned to death. After this, he set out with extreme passion to exterminate the young Christian religion.

"While they were stoning him, Stephen prayed, 'Lord Jesus, receive my spirit.' Then he fell on his knees and cried out, 'Lord, do not hold this sin against them.' When he had said this, he fell asleep. **And Saul was there, giving approval to his death.** On that day, a great persecution broke out against the church at Jerusalem, and all except the apostles were scattered throughout Judea and Samaria. Godly men buried Stephen and mourned deeply for him. **But Saul began to destroy the church. Going from house to house, he dragged off men and women and put them in prison.**" (Acts 7:59–8:3)

One day, during this time period, Saul decided to go to Damascus so that he could hunt down and arrest Christians.

"Meanwhile, Saul was still breathing out murderous threats against the Lord's disciples. He went to the high priest and asked him for letters to the synagogues in Damascus, so that if he found any there who belonged to the Way, whether men or women, he might take them as prisoners to Jerusalem." (Acts 9:1-2)

Saul (which was his Hebrew name) later changed his name to Paul (his Greek name). To the absolute shock and surprise of everyone, Paul suddenly became a devoted Christian, an apostle of Jesus Christ and, eventually, wrote thirteen books in the New Testament.

"What caused this change in Saul? What happened to cause a persecutor and an enemy of Christians to suddenly become one?"

Paul tells us what happened: "For what I received I passed on to you as of first importance: that Christ died for our sins…was buried…was raised on the third day…he appeared to Peter, and then to the Twelve…**and last of all he appeared to me also, as to one abnormally born**" (1 Corinthians 15:3-7).[230] Paul, the former church persecutor, not only had to convince non-believers that he had seen the risen Lord. He also had to convince the apostles and the new Christians. Acts 9:21 tells us, "When he came to Jerusalem, he tried to join the disciples, but they were all afraid of him, not believing that he really was a disciple."

Paul's belief that he had encountered the risen Christ was so strong that he, like the original apostles, was willing to suffer even to the point of death for the sake of his conviction that he had personally seen Jesus alive after the crucifixion. The fact that Paul suddenly converted from being a staunch opponent of Christianity to one of its greatest proponents, and was killed for this reason, is well-documented by early historians such as Tertullian (A.D. 160-220), Origen of Alexandria (A.D. 185-253) and Eusebius of Caesarea (3rd century church historian). They report that Paul was beheaded in Rome under the emperor Nero (A.D. 37-68) because of his Christian teachings. What would account for Paul suddenly changing his mind and becoming a member of the very church he had sought to destroy if not the resurrection of Jesus? Saul was not the only one who suddenly changed after encountering the risen Christ.

Consider the changed lives of the apostles!

When the mob "armed with swords and clubs" came to arrest Jesus, His apostles "deserted him and fled" (Mark 14:50). The apostle Peter not only deserted Jesus, but disowned and denied knowing Him three times. Matthew 26:74 tells us that Peter began to "call down curses on himself, and he swore to them, 'I don't know this man you're talking about.'" However, beginning just fifty days later, Peter and these same men boldly and courageously went everywhere transforming the Roman world with their message that Jesus was alive! These men became powerful leaders of the early church, and they remained steadfast in the face of imprisonment, suffering, torture, persecution, and martyrdom. Most of them, in fact, were eventually killed for their resurrection message. We only have to read the book of Acts to find that these disciples were willing to suffer for their belief that the risen Jesus had appeared to them. At times, these men were arrested, beaten, and sternly warned not to speak about Jesus and His resurrection. However, they would gallantly go right back out to the streets and preach that Jesus was raised from the dead and that they had personally seen Him alive.[231] Josh McDowell writes this about the apostles: "You could imprison them, flog them, kill them, but you could not make them deny their conviction that on the third day he rose again."

What ever happened to the apostles?

James, son of Zebedee, was killed with a sword (Acts 12:1-2). Early Church tradition and historians tell us that Matthew was also killed by a sword. Thaddaeus was killed by a spear. Andrew, Philip, Simon, Bartholomew and James, the son of Alphaeus were all crucified by the Romans. Thomas traveled to southern India to spread the gospel of Christ and was eventually pierced with a lance there. John was exiled to the island of Patmos (Revelation 1:9).

What about Peter?

Origen (A.D. 185-253) reports that Peter was "crucified head downward, for he had asked that he might suffer that way." In other words, he felt unworthy to die in the same manner as his Lord, Jesus Christ.

Do you really think these men would die for a lie?

If the resurrection did not really happen, the disciples knew it. It is highly unlikely that you could find twelve men who would die for a false story that they themselves concocted. These men suffered and died for their testimony that they had *personally* witnessed Jesus alive. Chuck Colson put it this way:

> "Twelve powerless men, peasants really, were facing not just embarrassment or political disgrace, but beatings, stonings, execution. Every single one of the disciples insisted, to their dying breaths, that they had physically seen Jesus bodily raised from the dead. Don't you think that one of the apostles would have cracked before being beheaded or stoned? That one of them would have made a deal with the authorities? None did."[232]

Imagine how it would damage the credibility of Christianity if some of the supposed eyewitnesses to the resurrection eventually recanted and abandoned the Christian faith. An example of this can be found in Mormonism where six of the eleven witnesses to the golden plates (allegedly containing a message from God written in reformed Egyptian that would be translated into the *Book of Mormon* by Mormonism's founder Joseph Smith) eventually left the Mormon Church.[233] In constrast, when it comes to the eyewitnesses of Jesus' resurrection, the apostles' unanimous willingness to be persecuted to the point of death indicates that they sincerely believed that Jesus rose from the dead and had appeared to them.

Consider the changed life of James, the brother of Jesus.

The New Testament tells us that Jesus had at least four brothers and one was named James (Matthew 13:55, Mark 3:21, 31; 6:3-4, John 7:5). We also learn from the Bible that Jesus' brothers did not believe that He was the Messiah during His lifetime: "...even his own brothers did not believe in him" (John 7:5). Later, after Jesus had been killed, James became a leader of the Jerusalem church, which was the epicenter of ancient Christianity (Acts 15:12-21). He later wrote the letter that bares his name in the New Testament and was recognized as an apostle of Jesus Christ (Galatians 1:19). In fact, the apostle Paul ranked James right up there with Peter and John as "pillars" of the Christian church in Galatians 2:9. The first-century Jewish historian, Josephus, writing around A.D. 93, tells us that James, "the brother of Jesus who was called the Christ"[234] was stoned to death by Ananias, the high priest, because of his Christian teachings. James' martyrdom is recorded by several early Christian and non-Christian sources alike.[235]

What happened to cause this kind of transformation?

Again, we find our answer in Paul's letter to the Corinthians: "Christ died for our sins...was buried...was raised on the third

day... **Then he appeared to James**, then to all the apostles..."
(1 Corinthians 15:3-7).

Other Evidences That The Resurrection Really Happened:

1. The large number of witnesses

After Jesus Christ was publically killed, He appeared to a large number of people at many different times and in different places. He appeared to skeptics like Thomas, to unbelievers like James, and to enemies like Paul. Again, 1 Corinthians 15 tells us that Christ "appeared to more than five hundred of the brothers at the same time, most of whom are still living..." This letter to the Corinthian church was written and was being circulated during the lifetimes of the men and women who clearly saw Jesus alive after He had been killed. If anyone doubted the truthfulness of this letter, all they had to do was to find one of these five hundred people and ask them about their experiences. Consider the astounding amount of evidence. Throughout history, eyewitness testimony has proven to be extremely powerful in the courts of law. If you allowed each of these five hundred witnesses just 6 minutes to tell their story in a court of law, this would amount to fifty hours of eyewitness testimony from just one appearance of the risen Jesus. Considering this point, biblical scholar Norman Geisler brings up a thought-provoking question, "If the resurrection had not occurred, why would the apostle Paul give such a list of supposed eyewitnesses? He would immediately lose all credibility with his Corinthian readers by lying so blatantly."[236]

After Jesus was killed and buried, He appeared...

...to Mary Magdalene – John 20:10-18; Mark 16:9

...to the women returning from the tomb – Matthew 28:1-10

...to Peter later in the day – Luke 24:34; 1 Corinthians 15:5

...to the disciples on the road to Emmaus – Luke 24:36-43

...to the apostles, with Thomas absent – John 20:19-23

...to the apostles, with Thomas present – John 20:24-29

...to the seven by the Lake of Tiberias – John 21:1-23

...to more than 500 people at one time – 1 Corinthians 15:6

...to James – 1 Corinthians 15:7

...to the eleven apostles – Matthew 28:16-20

...to the apostles as he was taken up to Heaven – Acts 1:3-12

...to Paul – Acts 9:3-6; 1 Corinthians 15:8

...to Stephen – Acts 7:54-60

...to Paul in the temple – Acts 23:11

...to John on the island of Patmos – Revelation 1:10-19

J.N.D Anderson writes this concerning the testimony of the appearances:

"Think of the number of witnesses—over 500. Think of the character of the witnesses—men and women who gave the world the highest ethical teaching it has ever known, and who even on the testimony of their enemies lived it out in their lives. Think of the psychological absurdity of picturing a little band of defeated cowards cowering in an upper room one day and a few days later transformed into a company that no persecution could silence—and then attempting to attribute this dramatic change to nothing more than a lie. That simply wouldn't make sense."[237]

2. The silence of the Roman and Jewish leaders

The Roman and Jewish leaders were powerful and hostile to the Christian faith. If they successfully proved that the resurrection of Jesus was not true, they could have destroyed Christianity forever. In Acts 2, Peter stood up in front of a large crowd of Jewish people just 50 days after Jesus was killed and said,

"Men of Israel, listen to this: Jesus of Nazareth was a man accredited by God to you by miracles, wonders and signs, which God did among you through him, as you yourselves know. This man was handed over to you by God's set purpose and foreknowledge; and you, with the help of wicked men, put him to death by nailing him to the cross. But God raised him from the dead, freeing him from the agony of death, because it was impossible for death to keep its hold on him... God has raised this Jesus to life, and we are all witnesses of the fact." (Acts 2:22-32)

Why didn't the Jewish leaders stand up and insist that he was lying?

The answer is simply this: Jesus' body was not in the tomb. The empty tomb was there, in walking distance, for anyone to examine it. If Peter was lying, the people would have yelled, "Peter, you're out of your mind!" But, instead, what happened? Three thousand people were baptized in the name of Jesus Christ for the forgiveness of their sins that day, and the Christian church was born.

3. The Jerusalem factor

Consider where the resurrection story was first proclaimed.

Jesus was publicly executed in Jerusalem. The story that the tomb was empty and that Jesus had been seen alive was first proclaimed publicly in Jerusalem. Think about it, if you are going to tell a big lie, where should you not tell it? You should not tell it where people know it's a big lie! For example, suppose I decided to make up a story and was going around telling people that I was voted the Most Valuable Player during last year's World Series. Where would I not want to tell that story? I might get away with it for a couple of weeks in Latvia, but I would hardly get away with it in the city that hosted last year's World Series. Likewise, if you're going to make up a story about Jesus' being raised from the dead in Jerusalem and it's not true, where do you not tell it? Jerusalem! Yet, Christianity began in the very place it could most easily be stopped. It would have been impossible for Christianity to begin in Jerusalem if Jesus' body had still been in the tomb.

4. The rapid and massive growth of Christianity

It is a truly remarkable and unprecedented fact of history that the seemingly problematic story that "a man who was publicly killed came back to life" gained widespread and rapid acceptance. In less than sixty days after Jesus was killed, the Christian church had more than 3,000 members. Christianity then quickly spread all throughout the Roman world. Today, Christianity is the largest religion in the world.

5. Worship on the first day of the week

One of the Ten Commandments is to keep the Sabbath day holy (Exodus 20:8, 31:12-17, 35:1-3). The Jewish Sabbath day is Saturday.[238] At the time of Christ's death, the Sabbath was a 1,500-year old tradition and a sacred part of a Jewish person's life. A great number of the earliest Christians were Jewish people. Yet, over time, they began to worship on Sunday, the first day of the week, rather than on Saturday. What can account for the abrupt change in this deeply ingrained social and religious structure? Why would they break a 1,500-year old tradition that God Himself ordained? The only plausible answer is that the early Christians were worshiping on Sunday to honor the resurrection of Jesus. For centuries the Jewish people had held Saturday as a sacred day to symbolize God's completion of His work of creation. However, by changing the day of worship from Saturday to Sunday, the early Christians were suggesting that "there is something more important than the creation of the world—and that is, the resurrection of the world's creator!"[239]

6. The phenomenon of the Lord's Supper

From the beginning of the Christian church, the Lord's Supper (also called Holy Communion or the Eucharist) has been a memorial of Jesus' death (see Matthew 26:26-29; 1 Corinthians 11:23-26). However, we read in Acts 2:46 that this was a time of joy, hope, and happiness. The memory of the meal which led directly to the betrayal and brutal killing of Jesus, their Lord and friend, would have been unbearably painful. What transformed the sorrow of the Last Supper into the joy of the Lord's Supper? Answer: He is risen! (Matthew 28:6)

7. The symbolism and meaning of Christian baptism

From the birth of the Christian faith, baptism was recognized as symbolically reenacting the death, burial (going under the water and dying to the old sinful nature), and resurrection of Jesus Christ (rising out of the water to share a new, resurrected life with Christ). The New Testament explains that when a person believes and confesses that Jesus is Lord and Savior, repents of his or her sins and is baptized, he or she is united with Christ in His death and resurrection.

> "...don't you know that all of us who were baptized into Christ Jesus were baptized into his death? We were therefore buried with him through baptism into death in order that, just as Christ was raised from the dead through the glory of the Father, we too may live a new life. If we have been united with him in a death like his, we will certainly also be united with him in a resurrection." (Romans 6:3-5)

How are we to account for the ancient symbolism and meaning of Christian baptism if the resurrection didn't really happen?

Conclusion

One of the greatest strengths about the Christian faith is that it is a religion deeply embedded in well-documented history. The resurrection of Jesus Christ was a historical event—one that can be investigated, scrutinized, and verified. Two thousand years of attempts by critics to account for the known historical facts surrounding Jesus' death and resurrection by rival theories have failed. Thus, Christians can be assured, confident, and delighted that there are no good reasons for rejecting the Bible's claim that Jesus rose from the dead.

"He is risen; So what?"

The famous British philosopher and outspoken atheist, Cyril Joad once noted the following:

> "The most important question in the world is did Christ rise from the dead? No question is more important, because if true, we dare not fail to acknowledge its implications. If it is not true, and Christ is still in His grave, then the last enemy, death remains undefeated, the darkness of the tomb is all there is and Christ is proven a liar."

What are the implications of the resurrection of Christ? What difference does it make? Do those peculiar historical events outside Jerusalem some 2,000 years ago have any relevance for our lives today or are they simply a fascinating part of antiquity?

1) Because of the resurrection, we can know without a doubt that there is life beyond the grave.

I love the story of the young minister who was asked to speak at a funeral. He had never spoken at a funeral before and was quite nervous about it. In his preparation, he found that he was having trouble choosing the right words to say. He wondered which biblical verse would best convey the message of hope during this painful time. This was very much on his mind as he picked up his daughter from school. When his little girl got into the car, she rolled down the window and a bee flew in. The little girl was terrified and began to scream. The bee eventually landed on the young minister's arm and stung him, leaving the stinger in his arm. The bee, however, continued to swarm around the car and the little girl continued to scream. The father eventually calmed his daughter by showing her the stinger and saying, *"Don't be afraid. The bee can't hurt you now! The bee's power to bring you harm has been taken away."* At that moment, it occurred to the young preacher what he would say at the funeral. The next day at the funeral, he told the story about the bee. He explained that because

195

the bee stung him, it was powerless to hurt his child. Then, he turned to 1 Corinthians 15:55 and read,

> "Where, O death is your victory? Where, O death is your sting? The sting of death is sin, and the power of sin is the law. But thanks be to God! He gives us the victory through our Lord Jesus Christ."

He explained that death is the most powerful, terrifying, and painful weapon the devil's got. However, when Jesus was nailed to the cross, He took the stinger. He took the sting of death upon Himself and, because of this, nothing can hurt His children now. Even though death is still an enemy, it is a defeated enemy. Because of the cross, the devil's power to bring us harm has been ultimately taken away.

2) Because of the resurrection of Christ, we don't have to fear death.

It is profoundly significant that the first recorded words of Jesus after the resurrection were these: "Do not be afraid!" (Matthew 28:10). Hebrews 2:14-15 says the following about Jesus' victory over our greatest enemy:

> "Since the children have flesh and blood, he too shared in their humanity so that by his death he might destroy him who holds the power of death—that is, the devil— and free those who all their lives were held in slavery by their fear of death."

There is a well-known story from the Middle East about a man who was walking through the marketplace and, all of a sudden, felt someone brush against his shoulder. He immediately felt an eerie chill all over his body. When he turned around, he saw a terrifying sight. Horrified by what he saw, he turned and ran as fast as he could. When he returned home, the master of the house asked, "What in the world is the matter with you? I sent you to the market place to buy vegetables and you've come back home empty handed looking like you've seen a ghost." The servant frantically exclaimed, "Someone brushed up against me at the market place, I turned around and found myself staring face to face with the messenger of death. Please don't send me back there! I don't want to go back there. I don't want to stay here. I think he's looking for me." The master said, "I can see you are terrified. Don't worry. I will go to the marketplace. You take my horse and ride as far as you can. In fact, ride all the way to Samara and stay away from here for a few days. I'll send word to you when the messenger of death has left this place. So, the servant quickly jumped on the horse and rode as fast as he could to Samara. Meanwhile, the master went to the marketplace. As he was walking around, he spotted the messenger of death, approached him and inquired, "Why did you scare my servant like that?" The dark figure responded, "I didn't surprise him as much as he surprised me! You see, I have an appointment with him at Samara tonight. Frankly, I didn't know what he was doing here this afternoon."[240]

The point of this story is clear and thought provoking. You and I have an appointment with death. We can run as far and as fast as we want, but we are going to keep this appointment. The important question is, "Are we ready?" The fact that Jesus is the resurrection and the life means that we don't have to fear this appointment.

3) Because of the resurrection, we can live in hope!

The resurrection of Jesus Christ is not simply a matter of history, it is also a matter of future hope. This historical event is God's assurance that we can have forgiveness for the past, a new life in the present, and hope for the future. It is testimony that we can go to heaven and that something better is available for us than this present messed up world. The apostle Peter put it this way,

"Praise be to the God and Father of our Lord Jesus Christ! In his great mercy he has given us new birth into a living hope through the resurrection of Jesus Christ from the dead." (1 Peter 1:3)

Paul writes to assure us that when a Christian dies we do not need to mourn as others do, saying,

> "Brothers, we do not want you to be ignorant about those who fall asleep, or to grieve like the rest of men, who have no hope. We believe that Jesus died and rose again and so we believe that God will bring with Jesus those who have fallen asleep in him." (1 Thessalonians 4:13-16)

He also reminds us that the resurrection of Christ is the foreshadowing of the resurrection of his followers: "...if the Spirit of him who raised Jesus from the dead is living in you, he who raised Christ from the dead will also give life to your mortal bodies through his Spirit, who lives in you" (Romans 8:11).

4) The resurrection shows that Jesus of Nazareth was God among us.

The resurrection of Christ is not only the supreme fact in human history, but the ultimate proof that Jesus was who He claimed to be. It suggests a stamp of approval from God Himself and shows that God endorsed Jesus as the true Messiah. The resurrection cast a whole new light on Jesus' life, identity, ministry, teachings, and death. If God raised Jesus from the dead, then evidently He affirmed and agreed with all that Jesus did and taught. In other words, God was effectively saying *Yes* to all of Jesus' shocking claims, actions, and teachings.

5) The resurrection gave meaning to Jesus' death.

The events of the Sunday morning after the crucifixion gave a whole new meaning to the events of the previous Friday. The resurrection suggested that Jesus' death was no accident but instead was the climax of God's long-intended divine plan to rescue us, free us, and provide a way to be forgiven for our sins. Peter said it this way in his sermon just fifty days after Jesus was killed: "Jesus was handed over according to the definite plan and foreknowledge of God" (Acts 2:23). At the last supper, Jesus had spoken of "giving his life as a ransom for many" and His body being broken and His blood poured out for the "forgiveness of sins." The resurrection is testimony that He was telling the truth and that because of His death, we can have forgiveness, freedom, hope, and a new life.

6) The resurrection shows us that biblical Christianity is true.

When Jesus' critics asked Him for a miraculous sign to prove that He had exclusive authority from God, He said He would give them one—the resurrection.[241] According to Jesus, this miracle would be the ultimate test by which we could know if He were telling the truth or not. By being raised from the dead, Jesus of Nazareth clearly distanced Himself from any other religious leader who claimed to have a special revelation from God. If the resurrection of Jesus really happened, then we now know where to go to find answers to the big questions of life—questions about origins, meaning, morality, truth, and destiny.

A Christian missionary was once trying to get this point across in simple terms to a group of people who were followers of a different faith. He asked them to imagine that they were on a long journey trying to reach a certain destination and somewhere along the way they became desperately lost. As they traveled further, they came upon two men—one was dead, the other was alive. Then the missionary asked, "From which man would you ask directions?" They all laughed and agreed, "The living man, of course!" The missionary responded, "Why, then, do you let a dead man tell you the way to get to heaven?" G.B. Hardy famously summed it up this way: "Here is the complete record:

Confucius's tomb:	Occupied
Buddha's tomb:	Occupied
Mohammed's tomb:	Occupied
Jesus' tomb:	**EMPTY!"**

7) The resurrection is proof positive that God's judgment will take place.

With all the positive aspects of the truth of Jesus' resurrection, we should not overlook one sobering, solemn note. The resurrection is indeed a past event within history, but it also points forward to another event beyond history. In Acts 17:31, Paul warns the people of Athens that "[God] has set a day when he will judge the world with justice by the man he has appointed. *He has given proof of this to all men by raising him from the dead.*" In other words, the resurrection gives us proof and advance warning that there will be a judgment day, we will all be judged and we all need to be prepared.

The resurrection of Jesus is the cornerstone of Christianity. Without the resurrection of Christ, the whole Christian message of forgiveness, new life, and eternal hope ceases to make any sense. The resurrection is proof of Jesus' triumph over sin, evil and death. It is the miracle of all miracles and the fact that it really happened is a matter of reliable history. The resurrection of Christ serves as a vital piece of evidence for the existence of a powerful and loving God who is at work in human history. The empty tomb heralds God's moment of victory and testifies to His capacity to take suffering and evil and turn them into a means of divine blessing and victory. The historical event of the resurrection is God's assurance that there is life beyond the grave and that we can go to heaven to share in the joys of paradise that God has prepared for His people from the foundation of the world. It has been rightly said that God did not roll away the stone so that Jesus could come home; He rolled away the stone so that you could. Jesus made a glorious promise to his followers in John 14:19, "Because I live, you also will live." Do you believe this?

In the absence of valid historical evidence or compelling reasons for rejecting Jesus' resurrection, nothing prevents a rational person from concluding that Jesus' resurrection from the dead was a real event in history and that because He was raised from the dead, we, too, can be raised to live with God in heaven for eternity. In 1972, John Lennon wrote a personal letter to a minister. After quoting one of his famous lyrics, "Money can't buy me love," he said the following: "It's true. The point is this, I want happiness. I don't want to keep on with drugs... Explain to me what Christianity can do for me. Is it phony? Can He love me? I want out of hell." [242]

In 2005, Steve Kroft from *60 Minutes* interviewed the great NFL quarterback Tom Brady of the New England Patriots. In this interview, Brady said the following: "Why do I have three Super Bowl rings, and still think there's something greater out there for me? I mean, maybe a lot of people would say, 'Hey man, this is what is." I reached my goal, my dream, my life. Me, I think: 'God, it's gotta be more than this...'"

Steve Kroft asked, "What's the answer?"

Tom Brady responded, "I wish I knew. I wish I knew." [243] I wish that John Lennon and Tom Brady understood what Octavius Winslow (1808-1878) knew:

"The child of God is, from necessity, a joyful man. His sins are forgiven, his soul is justified, his person is adopted, his trials are blessings, his conflicts are victories, his death is immortality, his future is a heaven of inconceivable, unthought-of, untold, and endless blessedness—which such a God, such a Savior, and such a hope, is he not, ought he not, to be a joyful man...The religion of Christ is the religion of joy. Christ came to take away our sins, to roll off our curse, to unbind our chains, to open our prison-house, to cancel our debt... Is not this joy? Where can we find a joy so real, so deep, so pure, so lasting? There is every element of joy—deep, ecstatic, satisfying joy—in the gospel of Christ. The believer in Jesus is essentially a happy man." [244]

NOTES

1. This story was told by Lisabeth Foster who worked as a hostess/ tour guide for years at Helen Keller's childhood home in Tuscumbia, Alabama.

2. Aldous Huxley, *Ends and Means* (London: Chatto & Windus, 1946), 270-273.

3. Sundar Singh, *Wisdom of Sadhu* (Plough Publishing, 2000), 170. As cited in Joe Boot's *A Time to Search* (Eastbourne, England: Kingsway Publications, 2002), 250.

4. Ravi Zacharias, *Can Man Live Without God?* (Word Publishing, 1994).

5. Ravi Zacharias, *Can Man Live Without God?* (Nashville: W Publishing Group, 1994), 54.

6. Philip Yancey (General Editor), *The Student Bible – The New International Version* (Grand Rapids: Zondervan Publishing House, 1992), 722.

7. Ravi Zacharias, *Cries of the Heart* (Nashville: Word Publishing, 1998), 140.

8. Ravi Zacharias, *Is There Meaning in Evil and Suffering?* (Video: Faith and Science Lecture Forum, Ravi Zacharias International Ministries, 1999).

9. Philip Yancey (General Editor), *The Student Bible – The New International Version* (Grand Rapids: Zondervan Publishing House, 1992), 728.

10. Philip Yancey (General Editor), *The Student Bible – The New International Version* (Grand Rapids: Zondervan Publishing House, 1992), 723.

11. Sting, BBC Interview with Parkinson, July 30, 2001. As cited in Joe Boot, *A Time To Search* (Eastbourne: Kingsway Publications, 2002), 118.

12. Ravi Zacharias, *Can Man Live Without God?* (Nashville: W Publishing Group, 1994), 56. Taken from Alister McGrath, *Intellectuals Don't Need God* (Grand Rapids: Zondervan, 1993), 15.

13. Taken from Diane Sawyer's interview with Mel Gibson on ABC's *"Primetime Live"* which aired on February 16th, 2004.

14. Nicky Gumbel, *Questions of Life* (Colorado Springs: Cook Communications Ministries, 2004), 15.

**"What good is it for a man to gain the whole world,
yet forfeit his soul?"
~ Jesus Christ. (Mark 8:36)**

15. Tommy Nelson, *Navigating the Icebergs of Life* – An audio lesson series on the book of Ecclesiates - (Denton, TX: Media Ministry of Denton Bible Church, 2003).

16. William Barclay, *The Gospel of John, Vol. 1-The Daily Study Bible Series*, (Philadelphia: The Westminster Press, 1975), 155.

17. Philip Yancey, *Rumors of Another World: What on Earth Are We Missing?* (Grand Rapids: Zondervan, 2003).

18. Alister McGrath, *Glimpsing the Face of God*, 51, 53. As cited in Lee Strobel, *The Case for a Creator* (Grand Rapids, MI: Zondervan, 2004), 292.

**"A car is made to run on gasoline, and it would not run properly on anything else. Now God designed the human machine to run on Himself. He Himself is the fuel our spirits were designed to burn, or the food our spirits were designed to feed on. There is no other."
~ C. S. Lewis**

"I am the bread of life. Whoever comes to me will never go hungry, and whoever believes in me will never be thirsty." ~ Jesus Christ (John 6:35)

19. Augustine, *Confessions,* Book 1, Section 1, Paragraph 1.

20. This argument is often called "the cosmological argument" (*cosmos* means creation) or, more precisely, "the *kalam* argument."

21. This argument is known as the "argument from design" or "the teleological argument." The word *teleological* means "directed toward some goal" (*telos* means purpose).

22. Michael A. Corey, *The God Hypothesis* (Rowman & Littlefield Publishers, Inc., 2000), 25.

23. Lee Strobel, (quoting William Lane Craig), *The Case for Faith* (Grand Rapids: Zondervan Publishing House, 1998), 76.

24. Ravi Zacharias, *Jesus Among Other Gods* (Nashville: Word Publishing, 2000), 64.

25. Robert Jastrow, *God and the Astronomer* (New York: Warmer, 1978).

26. All Scripture quotations, unless otherwise indicated are taken from the Holy Bible: New International Version. NIV. Copyright 1973, 1978, 1984 by International Bible Society.

27. Lee Strobel, *The Case for a Creator* (Grand Rapids: Zondervan, 2004), 108.

28. This is one of the *Quinquae viae* (Latin: *Five Ways*) that Thomas Aquinas offered as proof of God's existence in his best-known work *Summa Theologica* (written between 1265 –1274).

29. Ravi Zacharias and Norman Geisler, *Who Made God?* (Grand Rapids: Zondervan Press, 2003), 23.

30. Stephen W. Hawking, *A Brief History of Time* (New York: Bantam Books, 1988), 123.

31. In fact, the size of the moon "just happens" to be 400 times smaller than the sun and the moon "just happens" to be precisely 400 times closer to the earth than the sun is. This "just happens" to make a total solar eclipse possible from an earthbound point of view whenever their orbital travels bring them in line with one another. *"One can't help but feel a nagging sense of suspicion that there is probably more going on here than just a mindless series of happy accidents."* (Michael A. Corey, *The God Hypothesis*, 142).

32. See: Patrick Glynn, "The Making and Unmaking of an Atheist." In: *God: The Evidence* (Rocklin, Calif.: Forum, 1997), 1-20. As cited in Lee Strobel, *The Case for a Creator* (Grand Rapids: Zondervan, 2004), 126.

33. Michael A. Corey, *The God Hypothesis* (Rowman & Littlefield Publishers, Inc., 2000), 11, 39.

34. Dr. Robin Collins, as cited in Lee Strobel, *The Case for a Creator* (Grand Rapids: Zondervan, 2004), 133-134.

35. Michael A. Corey, *The God Hypothesis* (Rowman & Littlefield Publishers, Inc., 2000), 46.

36. Michael A. Corey, *The God Hypothesis* (Rowman & Littlefield Publishers, Inc., 2000), 44.

37. Sir Fred Hoyle, "The Universe: Past and Present Reflections," *Annual Review of Astronomy and Astrophysics* 20 (1982).

38. As cited in Lee Strobel, *The Case for a Creator* (Grand Rapids: Zondervan, 2004), 78.

39. Cited in Lee Strobel, *The Case for a Creator* (Grand Rapids: Zondervan, 2004), 78.

40. Robin Collins, "A Scientific Argument for the Existence of God: The Fine-Tuning Design Argument." Cited in Lee Strobel, *The Case for a Creator* (Grand Rapids: Zondervan, 2004), 130.

41. Rubel Shelly, *Prepare to Answer - A Defense of the Christian Faith* (Nashville: 21st Century Christian, 1990), 72.

42. Richard Dawkins, quoted in Phillip E. Johnson, *Defeating Darwinism by Opening Minds* (Dover's Grove, IL: InterVarsity Press, 1997), 77.

43. Phillip E. Johnson, *Defeating Darwinism* (Downers Grove, IL: Intervarsity Press, 1997), 75.

44. Lee Strobel, *The Case for a Creator* (Grand Rapids: Zondervan, 2004), 78.

45. A quote from *Unlocking the Mystery of Life*, a video produced by Illustra Media.

46. Lee Strobel, *The Case for a Creator* (Grand Rapids: Zondervan, 2004), 225.

47. *Ibid.*, 244.

48. See Hugh Davson, *Physiology of the Eye – 5th ed* (New York: McGraw Hill, 1991).

QUOTATIONS ABOUT INTELLIGENT DESIGN

"For since the creation of the world God's invisible qualities—his eternal power and divine nature—have been clearly seen, being understood from what has been made, so that men are without excuse." (Romans 1:20)

"Does he who formed the eye not see?" (Psalm 94:9)

"If there is something in the world which human reason, strength and power are incapable of producing, that which produces it must be better than man. But the heavens and everything which displays unceasing regularity cannot be produced by man. Therefore that by which those things are produced is better than man. And what name rather than God would you give to this."
- Chrysippus, Stoic philosopher (280 – 206 BC)

"When we see some examples of a mechanism, such as a globe or clock or some such device, do we doubt that it is the creation of a conscious intelligence? So when we see the movement of the heavenly bodies... how can we doubt that these too are not only the works of reason but of a reason which is perfect and divine?"
- Cicero, De Natura Deorum (106-43 BC)

"The only incomprehensible thing about the universe is that it is comprehensible." Albert Einstein (1879–1955)

"It would be very difficult to explain why the universe should have begun just this way, except as an act of God who intended to create beings like us." - Stephen Hawking

"I think it's indisputable that there has never been a time in history when the hard evidence of science was more confirmatory of belief in God than today." - William Lane Craig

"Astronomy leads us to a unique event, a universe which was created out of nothing, one with the very delicate balance needed to provide exactly the right conditions required to permit life, and one which has an underlying (one might say 'supernatural') plan."
- Arno Penzias – Physics Nobel Prizewinner 1978

"I am intrigued by how the universe came into existence with the laws of nature already written into it." Outspoken Oxford Atheist, Richard Dawkins, when asked to "imagine for a moment that you were thinking about arguments that might make you change your mind (about his atheistic worldview)."

"In crossing a heath suppose I pitched my foot against a stone, and were asked how the stone came to be there, I might possibly answer, that for any thing I knew to the contrary it had lain there for ever; nor would it, perhaps, be very easy to show the absurdity of this answer. But supposing I had found a watch upon the ground, and it should be inquired how the watch happened to be in that place, I should hardly think of the answer which I had before given, that for any thing I knew the watch might have been always there. Yet why should not this answer serve for the watch as well as for the stone; why is it not as admissible in the second case as in the first? For this reason and for no other, namely, that when we come to inspect the watch, we perceive – what we could not discover in the stone – that its several parts are framed and put together for a purpose, e.g. they are so formed and adjusted as to produce motion, and that motion so regulated as to point out the hour of the day; that if the different parts had been shaped different from what they are, or placed after any other manner or in any other order than that in which they are placed, either no motion at all would have been carried on in the machine, or none which would have answered the use that is now served by it."
- William Paley (1743-1805)

49. As cited in Francis S. Collins, *The Language of God: A Scientist Presents Evidence for Belief* (New York: Free Press, 2006), 2.

50. Francis S. Collins, *The Language of God: A Scientist Presents Evidence for Belief* (New York: Free Press, 2006), 1.

51. *Ibid.*, 3.

52. *Ibid.*, 20-21.

53. *Ibid.*, 21-22.

54. *French Philosophers from Descartes to Sartre*, (New York: Meridian Books, 1961), 485.

55. Charles Darwin, *The Autobiography of Charles Darwin*, ed. Nora Barlow (W.W. Norton, 1958). As cited by Joe Boot, *Time to Search* (Eastbourne: Kingsway Publications, 2002), 100.

56. Joe Boot, *Time to Search* (Eastbourne: Kingsway Publications, 2002), 47.

57. Ravi Zacharias, *Jesus Among Other Gods* (Nashville: Word Publishing, 2000), 113.

58. C. S. Lewis, *Mere Christianity* (San Francisco: HarperSanFrancisco, 2001), 10.

59. *Ibid.*, 13.

60. *Ibid.*, 17-18, 24.

61. *Ibid.*, 29-30.

62. *Ibid.*, 30.

63. *Ibid.*, 31-32.

64. These statistics were from 2015 and found on *www.biblesociety.org.*

65. Quote from Ted Bergman in Josh McDowell's, *The New Evidence That Demands a Verdict* (Nashville: Thomas Nelson Publishers, 1999), 9.

66. These statistics were from 2015 and found on www.biblesociety.org.

67. Charles Dickens, cited by Joe Boot, *A Time To Search* (Eastbourne: Kingsway Publications, 2002), 145.

68. Adapted from Leon Morris's assessment of the Gospel of John in *The New International Commentary on the New Testament - The Gospel According to John*, (Grand Rapids: William B. Eerdmans Publishing, 1971), 7.

69. John Blanchard, *Why Believe the Bible?* (Darlington, England: Evangelical Press, 2004), 6.

70. J.I. Packer cited in John Blanchard, *Why Believe the Bible?* (Darlington, England: Evangelical Press, 2004), 21.

71. Norman Geisler, *How Can We Know the Bible Is the Word of God?* (International Students, Inc., 1995).

72. Ravi Zacharias, *Is There Meaning in Evil and Suffering?* (Video: Faith and Science Lecture Forum, Ravi Zacharias International Ministries, 1999).

73. Rubel Shelly, *Prepare to Answer* (Nashville: 21st Century Christian, 1990), 128.

74. Jean-Jacques Rousseau, cited by Joe Boot, *A Time To Search* (Eastbourne: Kingsway Publications, 2002), 145.

75. David Jeremiah, A Nation in Crises – *God's Plan for Leadership - Vol. 1"* (Atlanta: Walk Thru the Bible Ministries, 1996), 13.

76. Compare this with the *Qur'an* which claims (to use but one example of a questionable historical claim) that Alexander the Great (Zul-qarnain) was actually a Muslim and lived to a ripe old age (Sura 18:89-98).

77. Merrill F. Unger, *Unger's Bible Dictionary* (Chicago: Moody Press, 1971), 444.

78. Sir William Mitchell Ramsay, *The Bearing of Recent Discovery on the Trustworthiness of the New Testament* (London: Hodder and Stoughton, 1915; reprinted Grand Rapids: Baker Book House, 1953), 222.

79. Bert Thompson and Wayne Jackson, *A Study Course in Christian Evidences* (Montgomery, AL: Apologetics Press, Inc., 1992), 114 – 115.

80. Michael Licona, *Behold, I stand at the Door and Knock* (Alpharetta, GA: TruthQuest Publishers, 1998), 13. The Smithsonian's official statement may be obtained by request to: Anthropology Outreach Office, Department of Anthropology, National Museum of Natural History MRC 112, Smithsonian Institution, Washington, D.C. 20560.

81. *Ibid.* In fact, it is interesting to note that even professional Mormon archeologists from Brigham Young University (which is owned by the Mormon Church) will admit that archaeology and the *Book of Mormon*

are embarrassingly at odds with one another. For example, Dr. David Johnson, Professor of Anthropology at BYU states the following:

"What I would say to you is there is no archaeological proof of the *Book of Mormon*. You can look all you want. And there's been a lot of speculation about it. There've been books written by Mormon scholars saying that 'this event took place here' or 'this event took place here.' But that's entirely speculative. There is absolutely no archaeological evidence that you can tie directly to the events that took place." [Quoted from a personal telephone conversation between Dr. Johnson and Michael Licona – cited in Michael Licona, *Behold, I stand at the Door and Knock* (Alpharetta, GA: TruthQuest Publishers, 1998), 15.]

82. Josh McDowell, *The New Evidence That Demands a Verdict* (Nashville: Thomas Nelson Publishers, 1999), 90.

83. S. I. McMillen, M.D., *None of These Diseases* (New Jersey: Fleming H. Revell Company, 1973), 9.

84. "The Bible: The Believers Gain," *Time*, 30 Dec. 1974, 34. Cited in Rubel Shelly, *Prepare to Answer: A Defense of the Christian Faith* (21st Century Christian, 1990),103.

QUOTATIONS ABOUT THE BIBLE

"It is impossible to rightly govern the world without God and the Bible. He is worse than an infidel who does not read the Bible and acknowledge his obligation to God." - George Washington

"I have always said and always will say that the studious perusal of the Sacred Volume will make better citizens, better farmers, better husbands. The Bible makes the best people in the world." - Thomas Jefferson

"My custom is to read four or five chapters of the Bible every morning immediately after rising. It seems to me the most suitable manner of beginning the day. It is an invaluable and inexhaustible mine of knowledge and virtue." - John Quincy Adams

"I believe the Bible is the best gift God has ever given man. All the good from the Savior of the world is communicated to us through this book.

I am profitably engaged in reading the Bible. Take all of this Book upon reason that you can and the balance of faith, and you will live and die a better man." - Abraham Lincoln

"All things desirable to men are contained in the Bible." - Abraham Lincoln

"To every man who faces life with real desire to do his part in everything, I appeal for a study of the Bible." - Theodore Roosevelt

"A thorough knowledge of the Bible is worth more than a college education." - Theodore Roosevelt

"I have a very simple thing to ask of every man and woman, that from this day on they will realize that part of the destiny of America lies in their daily perusal of this great Book." - Woodrow Wilson

"Cultivate an acquaintance with and a firm belief in the Holy Scriptures. This is your certain interest." - Benjamin Franklin

"I have known ninety-five great men of the world in my time, and of these, eighty-seven were all followers of the Bible." - Douglas MacArthur

"If the Bible is not widely circulated among the masses in this country, I do not know what is to become of us as a nation. And the thought is one to cause solemn reflection on the part of every patriot and Christian. If truth be not diffused, error will be. If God and His Word are not known and received, the devil and his works will gain the ascendancy. If the evangelical volume does not reach every hamlet, the pages of a corrupt and licentious literature will. If the power of the gospel is not felt through the length and breath of the land, anarchy and misrule, degradation and misery, corruption and darkness will reign without mitigation or end." - Daniel Webster

"To what greater inspiration and counsel can we turn than the imperishable truth to be found in this treasure house, the Bible?" - Queen Elizabeth II

"We believe that [the Bible] contains the divine answer to the deepest needs of humanity, that it sheds unique light on our path in a dark world, and that it sets forth the way to our eternal well-being." –
The New International Version Committee on Bible Translation

85. Much of the discussion about the trustworthiness of the New Testament was inspired by a lecture conducted by Dr. Craig Blomberg in 2000 at Colorado State University. Dr. Blomberg is a professor of New Testament at Denver Seminary and the author of *The Historical Reliability of the Gospels*.

86. Lee Strobel, (quoting Bruce Metzger) *The Case for Christ* (Grand Rapids: ZondervanPublishingHouse, 1998), 59.

87. Norman Geisler and William E. Nix, *A General Introduction to the Bible* (Chicago: Moody Press, 1986), 123,124, 386.

88. This chart comes from Norman Geisler, *How Can We Know the Bible Is the Word of God?* (International Students, Inc., 1995).

89. Floyd McElveen, *God's Word, Final, Infallible and Forever* (Grand Rapids: Gospel Truths Ministries, 1985), 19.

90. Norman Geisler, *How Can We Know the Bible Is the Word of God?* (International Students, Inc., 1995). Quoting from Irenaeus, Adversus haereses 3.3.4.

91. Ibid., 33.

92. Lee Strobel, *The Case for Faith* (Grand Rapids: Zondervan Publishing House, 2000), 264.

93. Cornelius Tacitus, *Annals: Book 15*, edited by N. Miller (Bristol: Bristol Classical Press Latin Texts, 1998), 44.

94. Pliny the Younger, *Letters*, Book 10, Harvard Classics Series, translated by William Melmoth (New York: Collier and Son, 1909 – 14), Letter 96.

95. Although none of Thallus' manuscripts have survived, his writings are referred to in the writings of Julius Africanus (A.D. 221) who comments, "Thallus, in the third book of his histories, explains away this darkness as an eclipse of the sun – unreasonably, it seems to me." – Cited in F.F. Bruce, *The New Testament Documents: Are they Reliable?* (Leicester: IVP, 1964), 113.

96. Flavius Josephus, *The Antiquities of the Jews* (New York: Ward, Lock, Bowden, 1900), 18.3. This passage should be handled carefully because scholars are reasonably skeptical that Josephus - a non-Christian, Jewish writer – would have written about Jesus in such flattering terms (even going so far to say: "This man was the Christ"). Skeptics argue that early Christians may have added some pro-Christian sentences to Josephus' original. This certainly could be the case (although, this paragraph is found in the earliest existing copies of Josephus' *Antiquities*, and there is the possibility that Josephus wrote this passage about Jesus, but in a mocking tone). However, the passage still deserves our attention as it provides an important early historical reference to Jesus.

97. Nelson Glueck, *Rivers in the Desert: A History of the Negev* (New York: Farrar, Strauss & Cudahy, 1959), 31.

98. Thomas Watson (original from 1692), as cited by Joe Boot, *A Time To Search* (Eastbourne: Kingsway Publications, 2002), 145.

99. This list came from Samuel Davidson, *The Hebrew Text of the Old Testament* (London: 1856), 89.

100. Judson Poling, *How Reliable Is the Bible?* (Grand Rapids: Zondervan, 1998, 2003), 54-55.

101. This list came from the video entitled, *The Indestructible Book: The Story of the Bible*, Volume One, (Chandler, AZ: Bridgestone Multimedia Group, 2001).

102. See Deuteronomy 4:2; Jeremiah 26:2; Proverbs 30:5-6 and Revelation 22:18-19.

103. Dan Brown, *The Da Vinci Code* (New York: Doubleday, 2003), 234.

104. The Old Testament Apocrypha includes 15 books written between 200 B.C. to A.D. 200. Here is a list of these books:

   1) The First Book of Esdras
   2) The Second Book of Esdras
   3) Tobit
   4) Judith
   5) The Additions to the Book of Esther
   6) The Wisdom of Solomon
   7) Ecclesiasticus
   8) Baruch
   9) The Letter of Jeremiah
   10) The Prayer of Azariah and the Song of the Three Young Men
   11) Susanna

12) Bel and the Dragon

13) The Prayer of Manasseh

14) The First Book of Maccabees

15) The Second Book of Maccabees

105. Amy Orr-Ewing, *Why Trust the Bible* (Leicester, England: Inter-Varsity Press, 2005), 58-59.

106. Gleason Archer, *Encyclopaedia of Bible Difficulties* (Zondervan Publishing House, 1982).

107. Lee Strobel, *The Case for Christ* (Downers Grove, IL: InterVarsity Press, 1986), 137-138.

108. Joni Eareckson Tada and Steven Estes, *When God Weeps: Why Our Sufferings Matter to the Almighty* (Grand Rapids: Zondervan, 1997), 23-24.

109. Philip Yancey, *Where Is God When It Hurts?* (Grand Rapids: Zondervan, 1990), 9.

110. John Stott, *The Cross of Christ* (Leicester: InterVarsity Press, 1986), 312.

111. The area of theology concerned with the problem of suffering and evil has come to be known as *theodicy* which means "a vindication of the justice of God in establishing a world in which evil exists."

112. Henri Blocher, *Evil and the Cross* (Leicester: Apollos, 1994), 9.

113. The word *pantheism* comes from two Greek words πάν (or *'pan'*) meaning "all" and θεός (or *'theos'*) meaning God. Pantheism literally means "God is All"and "All is God." It is the view that everything (the universe or nature) and God are equivalent.

114. Ravi Zacharias, *Jesus Among Other Gods* (Nashville: Word Publishing, 2000), 118.

115. This description of the atheistic worldview came from L.T. Jeyachandran, a Christian lecturer from South India.

116. Ravi Zacharias, *Can Man Live Without God?* (Nashville: W Publishing Group, 1994), 182.

117. Ravi Zacharias and Norman Geisler, *Who Made God?* (Grand Rapids: Zondervan Press, 2003), 35.

118. Richard Dawkins, *Out of Eden* (New York: Basic Books, 1992), 133.

119. Ravi Zacharias, *Jesus Among Other Gods* (Nashville: Word Publishing, 2000), 114.

120. Norman Geisler, *Baker Encyclopedia of Christian Apologetics* (Grand Rapids: Baker Academic, 1999), 224.

121. John Stott, *The Cross of Christ*, 17.

122. Norman Geisler, *Baker Encyclopedia of Christian Apologetics* (Grand Rapids: Baker Academic, 1999), 221.

123. C.S. Lewis, *Mere Christianity* (San Francisco: HarperSanFrancisco, HarperCollins Edition, 2001), 47-48.

124. Blocher, *Evil and the Cross*, 128.

125. How do we know that angels have been created with the capacity to choose between good and evil? The Bible tells us in 2 Peter 2:4 and Jude 6 that some angels sinned and "abandoned their own home."

126. John Stott, *The Cross of Christ*, 313.

127. Blocher, *Evil and the Cross*,129.

128. John Blanchard, *Where Was God on September 11?* (Auburn, MA: Evangelical Press, 2002), 15.

129. C. S. Lewis, *The Problem of Pain – C.S. Lewis Signature Classics Edition* (London: HarperCollins Publishers, 2002), 33.

130. Norman Geisler and Ron Brooks, *When Skeptics Ask* (Wheaton, Illinois: Victor Books, 1990), 73.

131. *Ibid.*

132. On several occasions, the Bible states that the devil can have a hand in sickness, deformities, and disease (Luke 4:35, 39; 13:16; 18:11, 16; Acts 10:38; 2 Corinthians 12:7). Michael Green's comments are helpful to add here: "...the Bible which asserts the reality and power of Satan is no less clear that the devil is not an equal and opposite figure to God. There is no dualism here. The devil remains 'God's devil' as Luther called him. He is on a chain, albeit a long one. His eventual destiny is destruction, but in the meantime he is out to spoil God's world in every way possible." Michael Green, *Evangelism Through the Local Church* (London: Hodder & Stoughton, 1990), 199.

133. Joni Eareckson Tada and Steven Estes, *When God Weeps: Why Our Sufferings Matter to the Almighty* (Grand Rapids: Zondervan, 1997), 83-84.

134. John Blanchard, *Where Was God on September 11?* (Auburn, MA: Evangelical Press, 2002), 23.

135. Philip Yancey, *Where Is God When It Hurts?* (Grand Rapids: Zondervan, 1990), 18.

136. Joni Eareckson Tada and Steven Estes, *When God Weeps: Why Our Sufferings Matter to the Almighty* (Grand Rapids: Zondervan, 1997), 116.

137. C. S. Lewis, *The Problem of Pain* (New York: Macmillan, 1966), 138.

138. See Hebrews 12:5-11; Deuteronomy 28:15; Psalms 32:3-5; 38:1-8; 1 Corinthians 11:30; Psalm 107:17.

139. See John 9:1-3; Luke 13:1-5.

140. Joni Eareckson Tada and Steven Estes, *When God Weeps: Why Our Sufferings Matter to the Almighty* (Grand Rapids: Zondervan, 1997), 202.

141. The Christian lecturer, Michael Ramsden suggests "maybe we struggle with suffering so much in the West because we are so comfortable most of the time that we feel we don't need God. We don't rely on Him on a daily basis, and so we don't really know Him as we should. When suffering comes along, therefore, it is not so much that it takes

us away from God, but that it reveals to us that we haven't really been close to Him in the first place." Scottish theologian James S. Stewart brings up another important point, "it is the spectators, the people who are outside, looking at the tragedy, from whose ranks the skeptics come; it is not those who are actually in the arena and who know suffering from the inside. Indeed, the fact is that it is the world's greatest sufferers who have produced the most shining examples of unconquerable faith." – Warren W. Wiersbe, *Classic Sermons on Suffering* (Grand Rapids: Kregel Publications, 1984), 92.

142. In fact, "if we are indeed the random product of evolution then aggression and domination are in themselves good things, because at least they assure survival of the fittest." – Ravi Zacharias, *Cries of the Heart* (Nashville: Word Publishing, 1998), 214.

143. Blanchard, *Where Was God on September 11?*, 9.

144. Ravi Zacharias, *The Real Face of Atheism* (Grand Rapids: Baker Books, 2004), 62.

145. John Blanchard, *Where Was God on September 11?* (Auburn, MA: Evangelical Press, 2002), 15.

146. Michael Green, *Evangelism Through the Local Church* (London: Hodder & Stoughton, 1990), 196.

147. Joni Eareckson Tada, Heaven: *Your Real Home* (Grand Rapids: Zondervan, 1995), 53.

148. John Blanchard, *Where Was God on September 11?* (Auburn, MA: Evangelical Press, 2002), 24.

149. See Psalm 58:10-11.

150. Peter Kreeft, as quoted in Lee Strobel, *The Case for Faith* (Grand Rapids: ZondervanPublishingHouse, 2000), 43.

151. Ravi Zacharias, *Is There Meaning in Evil and Suffering?* (Video: Faith and Science Lecture Forum, Ravi Zacharias International Ministries, 1999).

152. Michael Green, *Evangelism Through the Local Church* (London: Hodder & Stoughton, 1990), 201.

153. Philip Yancey, *Where Is God When It Hurts?* (Grand Rapids: Zondervan, 1990), xi.

154. John Stott, *The Cross of Christ* (Leicester: InterVarsity Press, 1986) 335. See also the following verses: Matthew 1:23, 25:34-40; James 1:27 and Acts 9:4.

155. Adapted from John R. W. Stott, *The Cross of Christ* (Downers Grove. IL: InterVarsity Press, 1986), 336.

156. John 14:6

157. David Bowie quoted in *Sunday Times* magazine, September 25, 1999, as cited in Amy Orr-Ewing, *Why Trust the Bible?* (Leicester, England: InterVarsity Press, 2005), 31.

158. From Plato's *Theaetetus* (152a – 171d) as cited on *http://answers.org/apologetics/relativism.html*. Most scholars date this writing around 369-367 BCE. This date was found on *http://www.iep.utm.edu/t/theatetu.htm*

159. To show the absurdity of a statement like, "There is no such thing as truth," Michael Ramsden would often respond with the following comment: "When someone says there is no such thing as truth, they are saying that it is true that there is no such thing as truth, but if it is true there is no such thing as truth, then what they said is not true. However, if someone says there is no such thing as truth, and they believe what they are saying is not true, then, it is not true that there is no such thing as truth. Thus, they have said nothing but in a very complicated way." (Michael Ramsden)

160. Cited in Paul Copan, *True For You, But Not For Me* (Minneapolis: Bethany House Publishers, 1998), 75-74.

161. Alister McGrath, *Intellectuals Don't Need God and Other Modern Myths – Building Bridges to Faith Through Apologetics* (Grand Rapids: Zondervan Publishing House, 1993), 111.

162. John 1:14.

163. 1 Corinthians 15:3-4.

164. Sura 4:157.

165. Hebrews 9:27

166. Cited in Alister E. McGrath, *Christian Theology: An Introduction* (Oxford: Blackwell Publishing, 2001, Third Edition), 276.

167. Not to mention that there is certainly no consensus or universally accepted definition of the word *religion* in the first place. McGrath rightly points out that "definitions of religion are rarely neutral, but are often generated to favor beliefs and institutions with which one is in sympathy and penalize those to which one is hostile." Alister E. McGrath, *Christian Theology: An Introduction* (Oxford: Blackwell Publishing, 2001, Third Edition), 536.

168. Alister McGrath, *Intellectuals Don't Need God and Other Modern Myths – Building Bridges to Faith Through Apologetics* (Grand Rapids: Zondervan Publishing House, 1993), 114.

169. Michael Green, *But Don't All Religions Lead to God?* (Grand Rapids: Baker Books, 2002), 24.

170. As quoted in Lee Strobel, *The Case for Faith* (Grand Rapids: ZondervanPublishingHouse, 2000), 145.

171. Ravi Zacharias, "Questions and Answers at the University of Illinois," RZIM-DVD (Norcross, Georgia: Ravi Zacharias International Ministry, 2002).

172. Steve Turner, '*The Atheist's Creed'* in *The King of Twist* (London: Hodder & Stoughton Religious, 1992).

173. Steve Turner, 'Chance' in *The King of Twist* (London: Hodder & Stoughton Religious, 1992).

174. Alister McGrath, *The Twilight of Atheism* (New York: A Galilee book published by Doubleday, 2006), 230.

175. Philippians 2:6-8 – *The Holy Bible: The New Revised Standard Version* (Nashville, TN: World Publishing, 1997).

176. Isaiah 53:2-5.

177. Søren Kierkegaard, *Philosophical Fragments*, trans. Howard V. Hong and Edna H. Hong (Princeton, NJ: Princeton University Press, 1985), 26-28.

178. Joe Boot, *A Time to Search* (Eastbourne, England: Kingsway Communications Ltd., 2002), 199.

179. Qur'an, (Mary, V. 19)

180. Quoted in *Y-Jesus* (Vol. 2), (Orlando: Bright Media Foundation, 2005), 96.

181. Talmud: BT, *Sanhedrin*, 43a mentions "On the eve of Passover Yeshua was hanged... because he has practiced sorcery and enticed Israel to apostasy..." Ethelbert Stauffer, *Jesus and His Story* (Translated by Richard and Clara Winston — New York: Alfred A. Knopf, 1960), 9. Quoted in: Josh McDowell, *The New Evidence That Demands a Verdict* (Nashville: Thomas Nelson Publishers, 1999), 314.

182. Ibid.

183. Qur'an, (the Table V. 110).

184. Qur'an, (Surah 19:19-21).

185. This list would include nine traditional authors of the New Testament, another 20 early Christian authors, four heretical writers, and nine non-Christian authors (Josephus, the Jewish historian; Tacitus, the Roman historian; Pliny the Younger, a Roman politician; Phlegon, a historian and freed slave; Lucian, a Greek satirist; Celsus, a Roman philosopher; Suetonius, a historian; Thallus, a historian; and Mara Bar-Serapion, a prisoner. For more information on this see Gary R. Habermas and Michael R. Licona's excellent work, *The Case for the Resurrection of Jesus* (Grand Rapids: Kregel Publications, 2004), 126-129.

186. Tacitus, Suetonius, Velleius Paterculus, Pluarch, Pliny the Elder, Strabo, Seneca, Valerius Maximus, Josephus, and the biblical writer, Luke. For more information on this see Gary R. Habermas and Michael R. Licona's excellent work, *The Case for the Resurrection of Jesus* (Grand Rapids: Kregel Publications, 2004), 126-129.

187. Ravi Zacharias, *Jesus Among Other Gods* (Nashville: Word Publishing, 2000), 149. Quoted in Henry Parry Liddon, Liddon's Bampton Lectures 1866, (London: Rivingtons, 1869), 148.

188. Rubel Shelly, *Prepare to Answer* (Nashville: 21st Century Christian, 1990), 184-185.

189. Philip Schaff, *The Person of Christ* (American Tract Society, 1913).

190. Bernard Ramm, *Protestant Christian Evidences* (Chicago: Moody Press, 1957), 170-171.

191. Lee Strobel, *The Case for Christ* (Grand Rapids: Zondervan, 1998), 172.

192. Ibid., 267.

193. Floyd McElveen, *God's Word, Final, Infallible and Forever* (Grand Rapids: Gospel Truths Ministries, 1985), 40.

194. Peter W. Stoner, *Science Speaks* (Chicago, IL: Moody Press, 1969), 109. The American Scientific Association reviewed Professor Stoner's work and concluded, "The mathematical analysis…is based upon principles of probability which are thoroughly sound, and Professor Stoner has applied these principles in a proper and convincing way." (Stoner, *Science Speaks*, 5).

195. Max Lucado, *He Chose the Nails* (Nashville: Word Publishing, 2000), 96. Citing William Hendriksen, *Exposition of the Gospel According to John, of New Testament Commentary* (Grand Rapids: Baker Book House, 1953), 431.

196. Lee Strobel, *The Case for Christ* (Grand Rapids: Zondervan, 1998), 183.

197. Michka Assayas, *Bono: In Conversation with Michka Assayas* (Riverhead Books, 2005).

198. C. S. Lewis, *Mere Christianity –Fiftieth Anniversary Edition* (London: HarperCollinsPublishers, 2002), 52-53.

"Come, all you who are thirsty, come to the waters;
and you who have no money, come, buy and eat!
Come, buy wine and milk without money
and without cost.
Why spend money on what is not bread,
and your labor on what does not satisfy?
Listen, listen to me, and eat what is good,
and your soul will delight in the richest of fare.
Give ear and come to me;
hear me, that your soul may live."

(Isaiah 55:1-3a)

199. Jane Walmsley, *Brit-Think, Ameri-Think: A Transatlantic Survival Guide* (New York: Penguin Books), 1986.

200. This genre of still life art was called *Vanitas* which is Latin for "vanity" or "emptiness." The term originally comes from the opening verses of the book of Ecclesiastes.

201. Paul's first letter to the Corinthians is generally dated A.D. 54 or 55. We learn in Acts 18 that Paul went to Corinth "while Gallio was proconsul of Achaia" (Acts 18:12) and stayed there "for a year and a half, teaching them the word of God" (Acts 18:11). Thanks to an important archaeological discovery, we can now pinpoint when this took place. An inscription discovered at Delphi, Greece records that Gallio's proconsulship took place in A.D. 51-52. It is generally agreed by New Testament scholars that Paul wrote 1 Corinthians approximately three years after this.

202. 1 Corinthians 15:14-19.

203. This question came from Gary R. Habermas and Michael R. Licona's excellent work, *The Case for the Resurrection of Jesus* (Grand Rapids: Kregel Publications, 2004).

204. The precise dating of Jesus' crucifixion is not a simple matter. John's Gospel indicates that Jesus' last supper took place on the night before the official Passover (which would have been the 14th of Nissan on the Jewish calendar), while Matthew, Mark, and Luke seem to suggest that this meal *was* a Passover meal. Biblical scholars believe that there is no contradiction here, thinking that Jesus simply celebrated the Passover meal a day ahead of schedule (perhaps to show that this was His own distinctive Passover meal). If this is the case, then we are looking for a year in which the day before Passover coincided with the day before the Sabbath. This occurred in the year A.D. 33. This scenario and other factors have led many to conclude that A.D. 33 was the year of Jesus' death and resurrection.

205. Pentecost (meaning "the 50th day" in ancient Greek) was an important Jewish holiday commemorating the giving of the Law of Moses on Mount Sinai. According to Exodus 19:1, this event took place fifty days after the Passover (the night the Jewish people were freed from being slaves to Pharaoh).

206. C.F.D. Moule, *The Phenomenon of the New Testament* (London: SCM, 1967), 3. Cited in Ravi Zacharias and Norman Geisler, *Who Made God?* (Grand Rapids: Zondervan Press, 2003), 25.

207. Gary R. Habermas and Michael R. Licona in their book entitled *The Case for the Resurrection of Jesus* refer to this approach as the "minimum facts approach." This approach begins, not with the evidence found in the Bible, but with the data that are "so strongly attested historically that they are granted by nearly every scholar who studies the subject, even the rather skeptical ones." Gary R. Habermas and Michael R. Licona, *The Case for the Resurrection of Jesus* (Grand Rapids: Kregel Publications, 2004), 44.

208. "When Pilate, upon hearing him accused by men of the highest standing amongst us, had condemned him to be crucified..." Josephus, *Antiquities* 18.64. *Josephus in Ten Volumes*, vol. 9, *Jewish Antiquities*, Loeb Classical Library, Louis H. Feldman, trans. (Cambridge, Mass.: Harvard University Press, 1981).

209. "Nero fastened the guilt [of the burning of Rome] and inflicted the most exquisite tortures on a class hated for their abominations, called Christians by the populace. Christus, from whom the name had its origin, suffered the extreme penalty during the reign of Tiberius at the hands of one of our procurators, Pontius Pilatus." Tacitus, *Annals* 15.44 (c. A.D. 115).

210. "The Christians, you know, worship a man to this day—the distinguished personage who introduced their novel rites, and was crucified on that account." Lucian of Samosata, *The Death of Peregrine*, 11-13 (c. mid-second century).

211. "What advantage did the Athenians gain from putting Socrates to death? Famine and plague came upon them as a judgment for their crime. What advantage did the men of Samos gain from burning Pythagoras? In a moment their land was covered with sand. What advantage did the Jews gain from executing their wise king? It was just after that that their kingdom was abolished...the Jews, ruined and driven from their land, live in complete dispersion...the wise king...lived on in the teaching which he had given." Quoted by F. F. Bruce, *The New Testament Documents: Are They Reliable?* (Eerdmans Publishing Co., Fifth Revised Edition), 114. This letter written by Mara Bar-Serapion, provides one of the earliest non-Christian, non- Jewish references to Jesus. The writer of this letter was a Syrian who lived around 73 years after the life, death and resurrection of Jesus Christ. His famous letter which references the murder of the "wise king of the Jews" was written to his son, Serapion, from prison. The British Museum now possesses this Syriac manuscript, which reveals three important things: 1) Jesus was regarded as a wise king. 2) Jesus was murdered. 3) Jesus' teachings lived on after He was killed.

212. "...on the eve of the Passover Yeshu was hanged." Talmud, Sanhedrin 43a (probably late second century). Note: *Yeshu* is Hebrew for Jesus and "hanged" is making reference to Jesus being hung on a tree, which was a Jewish way of describing crucifixion. In Galatians 3:13, Paul quotes from Deuteronomy 21:23 and describes the crucifixion of Jesus in Jewish terms by saying, "Christ redeemed us from the curse of the law by becoming a curse for us, for it is written: 'Cursed is everyone who is hung on a tree.'"

213. Bishop Eusebius of Caesarea, *Epistle of the Church in Smyrna* – as quoted in Josh McDowell, *The New Evidence That Demands a Verdict* (Nashville: Thomas Nelson Publishers, 1999), 221.

214. Quote from Albert Réville cited in Leon Morris, *The Gospel According to John – The New International Commentary on the New Testament* (Grand Rapids: Wm. B. Eerdmans Publishing Co., 1971), 805 – 806.

215. The practice of "finishing off" a crucifixion victim by spearing him is reported and verified by the Roman author, Quintilian (A.D. 35 – 95), in *Declarationes Maiores* 6:9.

216. William D. Edwards et al., "On the Physical Death of Jesus Christ," *Journal of the American Medical Association* (21 March 1986): 1463. Cited in Ravi Zacharias and Norman Geisler, *Who Made God?* (Grand Rapids: Zondervan Press, 2003), 98.

217. Gary R. Habermas and Michael R. Licona, *The Case for the Resurrection of Jesus* (Grand Rapids: Kregel Publications, 2004), 103.

218. "The punishment for falling asleep while on guard duty was death, according to the Roman laws." (Dion. Hal, *Antiquities Rom.* VIII. 79). As quoted in Josh McDowell, *The New Evidence That Demands a Verdict* (Nashville: Thomas Nelson Publishers, 1999), 237.

219. Josh McDowell, *The New Evidence That Demands a Verdict* (Nashville: Thomas Nelson Publishers, 1999), 239.

220. Albert Roper, as quoted in Josh McDowell, *The New Evidence That Demands a Verdict* (Nashville: Thomas Nelson Publishers, 1999), 248.

221. Merrill C. Tenney, as quoted in Josh McDowell, *The New Evidence That Demands a Verdict* (Nashville: Thomas Nelson Publishers, 1999), 261.

222. Paul's martyrdom most likely occurred in A.D. 64, the year Rome was burned. According to the early second century, Roman historian Tacitus, when the people blamed Nero for the fire, Nero fastened the blame on the early Christians and thus began a horrible period of brutal persecutions. For a detailed description of this, see Tacitus, *The Annals*, www.classics.mit.edu/Tacitus/annals.html. The historical fact that Paul was martyred for his Christian faith is further supported by the following early writing:

"That Paul was beheaded has been written in their own blood. And if a heretic wishes his confidence to rest upon a public record, the archives of the empire will speak, as would the stones of Jerusalem. We read the lives of the Caesars: At Rome, Nero was the first who stained with blood the rising faith. Then is Peter girt by another, when he is made fast to the cross." – Recorded by Tertullian (c. A.D. 200) – Cited in Gary R. Habermas and Michael R. Licona, *The Case for the Resurrection of Jesus* (Grand Rapids: Kregel Publications, 2004), 58.

In other words, Tertullian is saying that if you do not want to accept the Christian testimony concerning the martyrdoms of Paul and Peter, then you can find the same information in the official Roman public records.

223. There are several reasons to conclude that Paul was quoting an early Christian creed in 1 Corinthians 15:1-8. First, Paul begins this section of his letter by saying, "For what I *received* I passed on to you." Second, the passage contains the Aramaic name for Peter (Cephas) rather than the Greek name, which indicates early origin. Third, in the original Greek, the passage displays stylized parallelism (much like a poem or a song developed for easy memorization).

224. Clement of Rome, a contemporary of the apostles, wrote the following around A.D. 95: "Therefore, having received orders and complete certainty caused by the resurrection of our Lord Jesus Christ and believing in the Word of God, they went with the Holy Spirit's certainty, preaching the good news that the kingdom of God is about to come." – First Clement 42:3, Cited in Gary R. Habermas and Michael R. Licona, *The Case for the Resurrection of Jesus* (Grand Rapids: Kregel Publications, 2004), 54.

Origen (c. A.D.185 – c. A.D. 254) wrote, "Jesus, who has both once risen Himself, and led His disciples to believe in His resurrection, and so thoroughly persuaded them of its truth, that they show to all men by their sufferings how they are able to laugh at all the troubles of life, beholding the life eternal and the resurrection clearly demonstrated to them both in word and deed." – Origen, *Contra Celsum*, 2.56 in Roberts, Donaldson, and Coxe, eds. and trans., *The Ante-Nicene Fathers*.

Origen also wrote that "Peter had been crucified upside down and that Paul had been martyred in Rome under Nero." – Origen's commentary on Genesis, volume 3, which is cited by Eusebius (c. A.D. 262 – c. A.D. 339), *Ecclesiastical History* 3.1. This information was found in Gary R. Habermas and Michael R. Licona, *The Case for the Resurrection of Jesus* (Grand Rapids: Kregel Publications, 2004), 58.

All of these sources, biblical and non-biblical alike, affirm the disciples' willingness to suffer and die for their faith.

225. Polycarp (c. A.D. 69 – c. A.D. 155), *To the Philippians* 1:2; 2:1-2; 9:2; 12:2 (written around A.D. 110). Irenaeus (writing around A.D. 185) reported the following about Polycarp: "...Polycarp also was not only instructed by apostles, and conversed with many who had seen Christ, but was also, by apostles in Asia, appointed bishop of the Church in Smyrna, whom I also saw in my early youth, for he tarried a very long time, and, when a very old man, gloriously and most nobly suffering martyrdom, departed this life, having always taught the things which he had learned from the apostles." Irenaeus, *Against Heresies*, 3:3-4. As cited in Gary R. Habermas and Michael R. Licona, *The Case for the Resurrection of Jesus* (Grand Rapids: Kregel Publications, 2004), 54.

226. C.S. Lewis, *Miracles* (New York: Macmillan and Co, 1947).

227. Ahmadiya Muslims say that after Jesus escaped the cross He fled to India and is buried in Srinagar, Kashmir.

228. Frog and Amy Orr-Ewing, *Holy Warriors – A Fresh Look at the Face of the Extreme Islam* (Bletchley, Milton Keynes, Bucks, UK: Authentic Media, 2002), 15.

229. If you would like to read more about how this happened, you can find Paul's remarkable conversion story in the book of Acts 9:3-22.

230. For one example of this, see Acts 5:17-42.

231. Charles Colson, "An Unholy Hoax? The Authenticity of Christ," *BreakPoint* syndicated column 020329, (29 March 2002). Cited in Gary R. Habermas and Michael R. Licona's, *The Case for the Resurrection of Jesus* (Grand Rapids: Kregel Publications, 2004), 94.

232. For more information about the credibility problems of Mormonism, see Michael Licona's insightful book entitled "What to Say to Mormons & Jehovah's Witnesses When They Knock on Your Door." This book is available for free from the following website: *www.risenjesus.com.*

233. Josephus, *Antiquities* 20:200.

234. Eusebius (c. A.D. 262 – c. A.D. 339) is often called the first church historian. Writing about the martyrdom of James, the brother of Jesus, Eusebius cites Josephus (who wrote around A.D. 95), Hegesippus (writing around A.D. 165-175), and Clement of Alexandria (writing about A.D. 200). Eusebius, *Ecclesiastical History* 2.23, written around A.D. 325.

235. Norman L. Geisler and Frank Turek, *I Don't Have Enough Faith to Be an Atheist* (Wheaton, IL: Crossway, 2004), 243.

236. J.N.D. Anderson, "The Resurrection of Jesus Christ," *Christianity Today.* March 29, 1968. Cited in Josh McDowell, *Evidence That Demands a Verdict, Vol. 1* (San Bernardino, CA: Here's Life Publishers, Inc.), 224.

237. More precisely, the traditional Jewish Sabbath was observed from sundown on Friday until the appearance of three stars in the sky on Saturday night.

238. Quote from Michael Green's lecture entitled "Following the Authentic Jesus: Risen from the Grave" presented at the Friends of Wycliffe Hall 2010 Winter Conference on February 26, 2010.

239. Story told often by Dr. Ravi Zacharias.

240. During His life, Jesus claimed on several occasions that He would be crucified and then resurrected from the dead (Matthew 12:38-40, 16:21, 17:22-23, 20:18-19, 26:32, 27:63; Mark 8:31-9:1, 9:10, 9:31, 10:32-34, 14:28, 14:58; Luke 9:22-27 and John 2:19-22, The Gospel of John Chapters 14-16). Regarding these astonishing claims, Wilber Smith once commented, "...when Jesus said that he would rise again from the dead, the third day after he was crucified, he said something that only a fool would dare say, if he expected longer the devotion of any disciples, unless – he was sure he was going to rise. No founder of any world religion known to men ever dared say a thing like that!"

241. Steve Turner, *The Gospel According to the Beatles* (Louisville, KY: John Knox, 2006), 187-188.

242. Tom Brady, interview by Steve Kroft, 60 Minutes, CBS News, November 6, 2005, http://www.cbsnews.com/news/transcript-tom-brady-part-3/.

243. Octavius Winslow, "The Sympathy of Christ with Spiritual Joy," The Sympathy of Christ with Man.

A Personal Note
to Those in Search of God

On August 12th, 2000, a terrifying tragedy played out at the bottom of the Barents Sea (located north of Norway and Russia in the Arctic Ocean). After a series of explosions, a giant Russian nuclear powered submarine called the K-141 KURSK drifted to the bottom of the sea. Most of the one hundred and eighteen sailors on board were instantly killed. However, tapping noises detected in the icy waters and, later, a note in the pocket of Lieutenant Kolesnikov revealed that at least twenty-three men remained alive after the initial explosions. These sailors were trapped aboard with little hope and no means of communication to the outside world. It is almost unbearable to think about what these men were experiencing. Yet, think about this for a moment. Imagine the overwhelming joy those men would have felt if they heard a voice from the outside through radio transmission saying, "It's going to be all right. I know you're down there and I know what you're going through. Don't worry! I'm going to try to save you. I've sent someone down to help you and to get you. Listen to what he says, follow his instructions and you will live." Imagine the jubilant cheering that would have followed that message.

Some of your professors, friends, and peers will try to convince you that our universe is just like that submarine. They will try to convince you that we live in a closed system called the universe, and we are drifting aimlessly through space without any meaning, purpose, or ultimate destination. They will tell you that there is no voice out there to speak to us, comfort us, help us, or guide us. They will try to convince you that there is no hope for life outside this system. They will claim that we are on our own and our few days in this world is all we have.

Don't be deceived. God is and He has spoken. There is a voice from outside this system and that voice has said, *"It's going to be all right. I know you're down there and I know what you are going through. Don't worry! I'm going to try to save you. I've sent someone down to help you and to get you. Listen to what He says, follow His instructions and you will live."*

That someone is Jesus Christ, and there should be great rejoicing because of that message.

That very voice may be calling you today to become a Christian or to recommit your life to Him. If that is the case, please don't ignore this voice. Listen to what He says, follow His instructions, and you will find forgiveness for the past, an abundant life in the present, and hope for the future.

May God's richest blessings be upon your life!

HAVE YOU EVER WONDERED?